Tea Times at Lake Tahoe

A collection of recipes and golf tips from the Incline Village Golf Club.

Additional copies of this book may be obtained by addressing:

The Tea Times Press
P. O. Box 3414
Incline Village, NV 89450

For your convenience, order blanks are included in the back of the book.

Cover Artist, Barbara Kallestad

Copyright © 1996
Tea Times Press
Incline Village, Nevada

First Edition
First Printing: 3,000 copies June, 1996

ISBN: 0-9653473-0-3

Printed in the United States of America

Clip art images provided by Image Club Graphics, Inc.
and Corel Corporation.

Tea Times at Lake Tahoe is dedicated to the founding members of the
Incline Village Golf Club....

It was compiled in celebration of the Club's 25th Anniversary. The Club's
proud history began in 1971, and it is composed of 100 members who have
a sincere interest in the game of golf. After enjoying 25 summers playing the
game high in the Sierras in Incline Village we want to give something back
to the community we love. All of the proceeds realized from the sale of this
book will be returned to the community through contributions to various local
charities.

Cookbook Committee

Chairman & Editor — Helen DiZio
Cookbook Coordinator — Julie Clark
Testing Coordinator — Joyce Anderson
Publishing — Erin Scheller
Historian — Ann Tiller
Cover Design — Trary Bishop
Page Design — Julie Clark
Wines — Ron Stanger
LPGA & PGA Profiles — Chuck Otto
Jeanne Otto

Editing — Cynthia Silman
Bev Atherton
Trary Bishop

Advisors — Gayle McGough
Jean Teipner
Susie Anderson

Testing Committee

Katie Dimick	Alice Colling	Mabelle Kiper
Bev Atherton	Shiela Lonie	Barbara Kerber
GJ Kosanke	Karen Leonardini	Rockee Coalson
Steve DiZio	Sharon Valerio	Valerie Bowles
Marge Steil	Pat Stampfli	June Pulver
Helen DiZio	Julie Clark	Gayle McGough
Jean Teipner	Ann Tiller	Erin Scheller
Trary Bishop	Susie Anderson	Louise Shulman
	Beverly Hughes	

Thank you to all who spent countless hours working on this project.

Table of Contents

   Designates recipes with reduced-fat ingredients.

Contributing Golf Professionals

Patty Sheehan	George Archer	Arnold Palmer
Hale Irwin	Betsy King	Julie Inkster
Susie Maxwell Berning	Tom Weiskopf	Kay McMahon
Ellie Gibson	Lori West	Katie Peterson-Parker
Marta Figueras-Dotti	John Hughes	Shelly Godeken-Wright
Dale Shaw	George Bayer	

Patty Sheehan, whom we claim as our own, is Reno's all-time favorite sports figure. Patty has had a fabulous career since joining the LPGA in 1980 including 34 career victories (make that 35 as she just won the 1996 25th Anniversary Nabisco Dinah Shore). She has amassed over $5 Million in career earnings, won the LPGA Championship 4 times and the U.S. Women's Open twice and qualified for the LPGA Hall of Fame in 1993. Since 1981 Patty has won a tournament in 15 of the 16 years. She has shot a low round of 63 and has had 3 holes-in-one on the LPGA Tour. At the age of 13 Patty was rated one of the top junior skiers in the country. We're glad that Patty stayed with golf as she has become one of the all-time best golfers on the Women's circuit.

George Archer and his wife, Donna, are no strangers to Incline Village as they call it home. When not out on the driving range, playing the Championship Course, or practicing putting in the evening hours on the 11th Green, George can usually be found pursuing his favorite pastime—fishing. However, he goes to work most of the time on the Senior PGA Tour where he has logged 17 victories and 5 consecutive top 10 finishes. Prior to going to the Seniors, he had a very successful career on the regular tour with 12 winning efforts including the Masters in 1969. In total George has won more than $6 Million in his very successful career.

Susie Maxwell Berning. 1995 marked Susie's 32nd year on the LPGA Tour! She was named Rookie of the Year in 1964 and since then has amassed a very enviable record including 11 tour wins and 3 U.S. Opens. In 1989 Susie and her daughter Robin became the first mother and daughter duo to compete in the same event. Susie now lives in Hawaii but was a Nevada resident for many years. She was inducted into the Nevada Sports Hall of Fame in 1992 and the National Golf Coaches Association Hall of Fame in 1986. However, our favorite part of Susie's history is the years she spent as a member of the Incline Village Golf Club.

Arnold Palmer was the very first respondent to our request for support. We thank him for taking time from his busy schedule to share his favorite recipe with us. Arnold's career began on the PGA Tour 32 years ago. During that time he has amassed one of the most successful careers of all time. Amongst his accomplishments are 89 victories world-wide; he has won both the U.S. Open and the Senior Open and has won 7 majors including 4 Masters, 2 British Opens and 1 U.S. Open. He has won the Vardon Trophy 4 times, played on 6 Ryder Cup Teams, and participated in 40 U.S. Opens! He still attracts "Arnie's Army" and has even shot his age.

Hale Irwin has spent 27 very productive years on the PGA Tour during which time he has earned 20 first place finishes including 3 U. S. Open titles. He has played on 5 Ryder Cup teams and represented the U. S. twice in World Cup play. In 1995, Hale's first season on the Senior Tour, he was voted Rookie of the Year with victories and finishes in the top 12 in every event. Hale is a true athlete as he was the 1967 NCAA champion in golf at the University of Colorado and also a two-time All-Big Eight selection as a football defensive back.

Julie Inkster is a veteran of the LPGA having joined in 1983. In just her 5th event she captured her first tour win. Since then she has posted 14 additional wins including the Nabisco Dinah Shore twice, the Atlantic City Classic twice, and the Crestar Classic twice. She has shot 64 twice and has earned over $2 Million. Like many of the tour professionals, Julie participates in athletics of all kinds, basketball, racquetball, fishing, and skiing. She is married, has two daughters and lives in Northern California when not on tour.

Marta Figueras-Dotti was born in Madrid, Spain. Marta is the first Spanish woman professional golfer. She began playing golf at age 8. Early in her career she won numerous European titles including the 1975 and 1977 European Amateur, the 1979 Spanish and Junior Amateur, and she was a member of the Spanish World Cup Team from 1978-1992. She was an All-American at USC in 1982. She joined the LPGA in 1983 and logged 8 top 10 finishes in her rookie season. She has one career victory (1994), has earned over $1 Million, has 4 holes-in-one, and has shot 65 three times.

Tom Weiskopf was one of the more dominant players on the PGA Tour for more than 2 decades, winning 15 times. During one streak in 1973 he won 5 tournaments in an 8-week span!! Tom won over $2.2 Million on the PGA Tour before moving to the Senior Tour in 1994 where he won the first event he entered. He was runner-up at the Master's 4 times and runner-up at the U.S. Open. Tom is an avid hunter in the off-season, is a part-time golf analyst, and is actively involved in golf course architecture.

Betsy King joined the LPGA in 1977 and since then has become the Tour's leading all-time money winner—nearly $5.5 Million. She has 30 tour victories—quite a feat since she didn't win at all during her first 7 years on tour. From 1984-1989 she won 20 times! She has won the Women's U.S. Open twice, the Nabisco Dinah Shore twice, and the Women's Kemper Open twice. She's been a member of 3 U.S. Solheim Cup Teams, won the 1985 Ladies British Open and has earned 3 Rolex Player of the Year awards. With her 30th win in 1995 she gained entrance into the LPGA Hall of Fame.

Ellie Gibson joined the LPGA Tour in 1989 after competing on the Futures Tour. Prior to that she competed at Texas Christian University where she earned Academic Achievement Awards in 1986 and 1987 while earning All-American Honors for her golf accomplishments. Since joining the LPGA Tour, Ellie has won nearly $250,000 and has had top 20 finishes in several tournaments. She enjoys rollerblading, shopping, crossword puzzles and COOKING!

Katie Peterson-Parker says she will eat the same thing everyday if she is playing well. She began playing golf at the age of 7 and played on the University of North Carolina golf team and garnered All-American honors in 1988 and 1989. In 1990 she was a member of the Curtis Cup team and qualified for the LPGA where she began her professional career in 1990. She has won nearly $1/2 Million, $192,600 coming in 1995—her best year. Last year she had 4 top 10 finishes, including a 2nd place (lost in a playoff) at the Youngstown-Warren Classic. She also had her career best round at that event—65!!

Lori West attended Colorado University on an athletic scholarship in track and field where she competed in the Pentathlon. She did not start playing golf until age 22. She was runner-up in the 1979 Colorado State Amateur, played in just 4 other amateur events, then turned professional. Lori fired her career low round, 65 in 1989, posted her career-best finish at the 1992 Lady Keystone Open where she tied for second, recorded 5 top 20 finishes in 1993 and had a season stroke average of 72.09.

Kay McMahon began playing golf at age 6 on a course her dad made in their yard. She has played on the Women's Professional Golf Tour, American Golf Tour, in several LPGA tour events and in 3 USGA Women's Opens. She was the LPGA National Teacher of the Year in 1995. Currently, she is a teaching professional at the Lakes Country Club in Palm Desert, California, the Teaching Editor of *Golf for Women* magazine and hosts a radio program called *Golf Talk.*

George Bayer, the very first Golf Professional at the Incline Village Golf Resort, is retired and lives with his wife Mary Ann in Palm Desert, California.

John Hughes is a PGA Class A Golf Professional. He is a past President of the Sierra Nevada Chapter of the PGA and is currently the Director of Golf at the Incline Village Golf Resort in Incline Village, Nevada.

Shelly Godeken-Wright is a Class A PGA Golf Professional at the Incline Village Golf Resort. She is the Coordinator of the Fred Alexander Memorial Junior Golf Clinic at the Dayton Valley Country Club, in Dayton, Nevada. The clinic, one of the largest in the country, attracts over 1,000 kids and Hall of Famer Patty Sheehan is a Special Guest each year.

Dale Shaw, a former LPGA Touring Pro, is presently the Teaching Golf Professional at Indian Wells Country Club, a host course of the PGA Bob Hope Classic in Indian Wells, California.

Note From The Cookbook Committee

Tea Times at Lake Tahoe is a collection of over 250 selected recipes. Each recipe is a tried and true favorite of the contributor and has been tested and enthusiastically approved by a testing team. The recipes included are for cooks of all levels, from the very novice to the expert, and where possible we included recipes that use only the freshest ingredients. We have also included some recipes that are reduced in fat and are designated so with a heart symbol. We are very grateful to all Club members and their friends who shared their ideas, their recipes and their time. A special thank you to the LPGA and PGA Professionals who were so kind to donate their names, recipes and golf tips. We hope that this book enhances your culinary and golfing skills.

Measurements

2 pinches	=	1 bit
4 bits	=	1 smidgen
2 smidgens	=	1 dollop
3 dollops	=	1 gaggle
1 gaggle	=	2 glugs
2 glugs	=	1 blanket
3 blankets	=	1 smothering

Volume may vary with altitude.

About Lake Tahoe

- Lake Tahoe is 12 miles wide by 22 miles long and has a 72 mile shoreline of sandy beaches and rugged cliffs.

- At an elevation of 6,228 feet, Lake Tahoe is the second largest body of water in the world at that or any greater elevation.

- The drive around the lake is 77 miles and takes at least 3 hours.

- The average temperature of the water is 61 degrees and never varies more than three degrees either way.

- The lake's water is 99.7% pure. That is cleaner than the drinking water in most U.S. cities.

- In optimum conditions, one can drop a rock in the lake to a depth of 100 feet and still see it clearly.

- The lake is 1,645 feet deep at the deepest point. In other words, it is at least 5 1/2 football fields deep.

- Eight feet off the shore at Rubicon Point, one could drop the Empire State Building into the lake, stack the Washington Monument on top of it and the two would be completely immersed in water with 20 feet to spare.

- If Lake Tahoe were drained onto California, it would cover the entire state to a depth of 14 inches. Texas would be covered to 8 1/2 inches.

- If a Panama Canal were built all the way around the equator, the water from Lake Tahoe would fill it with enough left to fill a second canal from New York to San Francisco.

History of Incline Village

The portion of the Lake Tahoe basin called Incline Village was originally part of a 36,000 acre parcel of land owned by the eccentric multi-millionaire George Whittell. In 1959 an option was obtained from Whittell for 9,000 acres of the Crystal Bay, Nevada, property. In October of that year, on a gray, snowy day, Art Wood, a business man, and Bob McDonald, an attorney, viewed the property from a vantage point at the Mt. Rose lookout. The scene looked dismal but several days later Wood bought the property in the name of the Nevada Lake Tahoe Investment Corporation, a corporation formed by Wood and twelve other investors from a recent Hawaii venture. In June 1960, Harold Tiller (a member of the Incline Village Golf Club today) arrived from Oklahoma and he and Wood bought out the investors for $25,000,000.

They changed the name of the area to Incline Village. It was named for the Great Incline of the Sierra Nevada. In 1880, Incline was the site of ruthless logging to provide lumber for the great silver mines in Virginia City, Nevada. The Incline tram was built at the height of the logging to carry logs 4,000 feet up to the huge wooden flumes which carried the logs through the Marlette Tunnel. The base of the funicular was at the present Ponderosa Ranch parking lot.

In 1959, the original proposed plan for Incline Village was drawn by Ray Smith, an architect and land planner from Reno. In June 1960, tree fallers from Grass Valley came to Incline and cut the first trees for the first approved Subdivision called Ponderosa #1. On June 1, 1961, the Incline Village General Improvement District (IVGID) was created under the laws of Nevada. In August, Crystal Bay Development Company sold $5,445,378 worth of bonds to pay for sewer and water systems for domestic use and fire protection, streets and roads. That summer the General Master Plan was approved and lots were offered for sale starting at $10,000 - $39,000.

Two beaches, Burnt Cedar and Ski Beach, were reserved for community use. Since the property wanted for Ski Beach was not part of the original parcel bought by the Development Company, a new deal had to be negotiated. The property now known as Ski Beach was being leased from Mr. Whittell and was used as a trailer and camping park. The property was bought for what was considered at that time an outrageous price, $400,000.

Families that lived in Incline Village in 1960 saw a greatly different picture than what we see today. There was nothing above Highway 28, now

Lakeshore Drive, except for the "Old" Mt. Rose Highway, now Country Club Drive, and the new Mt. Rose Highway. That first winter there were only 5 or 6 other families that we knew of, living in Incline Beach in houses built on some 30 lots bought from Mr. Whittell before 1959, not part of Incline Village. Most of these homes were summer residences and not winterized. There were no schools, no grocery stores, no gas stations, nor anything else in Incline at that time. Kings Beach provided all of those necessities.

A single small snow plow kept Mt. Rose Highway clear of snow, consequently, the Highway was often closed for several days at a time. Children from Incline went to grade school in Kings Beach and high school kids went by bus to Truckee.

More capital was needed in 1962 and Art Wood and Harold Tiller took the former investors back into equity position; they could see that they had to build houses. Additionally, Wood and Tiller were avid golfers and thought a golf course would greatly enhance the recreation facilities offered for Incline Village. When they told investors they were planning an 18-hole Championship Golf Course and Clubhouse, they were met with great opposition. The investors said Wood and Tiller were on a "champagne diet with a beer income," and they said they would approve a 9-hole course and a temporary clubhouse in a trailer.

In 1962 one of the leading golf course architects, Robert Trent Jones, was asked to come to Incline Village to survey the area. Jones' enthusiasm knew no bounds. On his return to the offices of Crystal Bay Development Co. he stated, "The Incline Village Course would be one of the world's 3 most spectacular and interesting golf courses." Wood and Tiller got their way and construction began. John Uhalde, Field Superintendent for Incline Village was the managing engineer for the course and his crews worked summer and winter with some of the largest and most rugged machines made to clear the land. Frozen ground had to be cut to the depth of 2 feet at times to move boulders and to lay sewer and water systems.

The Tahoe Daily Tribune reported in 1963 that "the Clubhouse for the golf course located near the practice range is in the design stages and construction will begin soon." The Incline Village Golf Course opened in June 1964 with the Harrah's Men's Invitational Tournament and all golf course lots were sold by the time the course was completed. Ann Tiller and Juanita Wood organized the first Ladies golf, bridge, luncheon and style show in the new clubhouse called the Chataux. Art Wood originally thought the course would be too difficult for women golfers but the women golfers proved him wrong. The history of the course began on a good note when on opening day the first hole-in-one was made during the Harrah's Tournament and a Rolls Royce was awarded to the winner. The early 1960's were exciting times for Cal-Neva Lodge in Crystal Bay. Built in 1926, it was one of the earliest casinos on the North Shore. Through numerous sales and owners, the Lodge eventually ended up in the hands of Frank Sinatra in 1960 and it was opened again that summer. The exciting days of movie stars, top entertainers, the Kennedy family and a procession of Sinatra guests were enjoyed by guests of the hotel and by the North Shore residents. Some of the entertainers in the newly remodeled Celebrity Showroom were Dean Martin, Sammy Davis, Jr., Vic Damone, Eddie Fisher, Ella Fitzgerald, Juliet Prowse, Mickey Rooney, Lena Horn, Victor Borge, Gary Morton, Tony Bennett and many others. Some of them were golfers and were seen on the golf course.

In 1963, the McGuire Sisters also appeared in the showroom at Cal-Neva. A friend of Phyllis McGuire, Sam Giancana, who was listed in the Nevada Black Book of persons not allowed in Nevada casinos, was known to be "visiting" Phyllis at the Cal-Neva. Sinatra was ordered by the Nevada Gaming Commission to close the casino and when he closed for the winter it was closed forever for Sinatra at Cal-Neva. That was the end of an exciting era for the North Shore of Nevada.

The first hotel in Incline, The Sierra Tahoe was built in 1963 by Pacific Bridge. After numerous name changes, remodeling and rebuilding, the Hyatt has become a welcomed addition to Incline. The next few years saw much building of schools, a sewer plant, commercial buildings, condos, and houses, etc. Building also began on Ski Incline. The facility opened for business on Thanksgiving Day in 1966.

The TV show "Bonanza" came to the North Shore in 1959 to film locations for the new show. The stars and crew continued to come back to film outdoor locations in the area of Incline, Spooner, Truckee, Zephyr Cove and on property owned by Joyce and Bill Anderson. The Andersons later negotiated with NBC and the series' actors in 1967 to use the Bonanza name and opened The Ponderosa Ranch, a resort that has become known worldwide.

In 1968 Crystal Bay Development Company sold all unsold property and recreation facilities except beaches to Boise Cascade Corporation. At the same time IVGID obtained the beaches through the sale of bonds, reserving them for the use of the Incline property owners. Art Wood said "We finished what we set out to do. Incline had become what we had envisioned in our eight-year plan."

Ann L. Tiller
1996

Breakfasts of Champions
Breads & Breakfasts

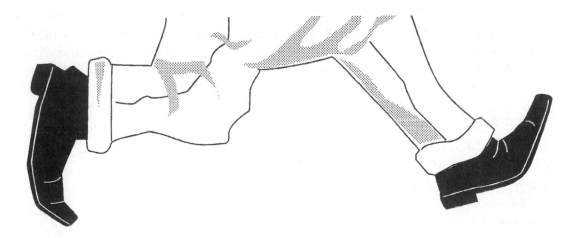

Breakfasts of Champions - Breads & Breakfasts

Crustless Crab Quiche

2 tsp. olive oil
1 onion, chopped
1 red Bell pepper, chopped
3/4 lb. mushrooms, sliced
2 large eggs
2 large egg whites
1 1/2 cups nonfat Cottage cheese
1/2 cup nonfat yogurt
2 TBS. white flour
1/4 cup grated Parmesan
1/4 tsp. ground red pepper
1/2 lb. lump crabmeat
1/4 cup grated Cheddar cheese
1/4 cup chopped scallions
1/4 tsp. salt
1/4 tsp. pepper

Preheat oven to 350º. Coat 10-inch pie or quiche dish with non-stick cooking spray. In non-stick skillet heat 1 tsp. oil over medium heat; add onions and peppers and cook 5 minutes. Transfer to mixing bowl; add remaining oil to pan, sauté mushrooms and add to onion mixture. In food processor or blender add eggs, egg whites, Cottage cheese, yogurt, flour, Parmesan, red pepper, salt and pepper and blend until smooth. Mix with vegetable mix, fold in crab, Cheddar and scallions. Pour into prepared dish. Bake 40 to 50 minutes until knife inserted comes clean. Let stand 5 minutes. Make in morning and serve after golf. Serves 6.

*When playing in a husband and wife tournament and you want to give your spouse some valuable advice remember to do it at the correct time....**only when they ask!***

Susie Maxwell Berning's Par Shootin' Pancakes

Contributed by
Susie Maxwell Berning
LPGA Professional

Susie Maxwell Berning was a member of The Incline Village Golf Club. She is a fabulous golfer and has had a great professional career with 3 U.S. Open Championships, in 1968, 1972 and 1973.

3 eggs
2 cups buttermilk
4 TBS. vegetable oil
1 1/2 cups flour
1 tsp. baking soda
1 tsp. salt
1 1/2 tsp. baking powder
1 TBS. sugar

Put eggs, buttermilk, and vegetable oil in a bowl and stir. Add dry ingredients and mix together. Ladle batter onto a hot griddle and cook on 1 side until bubbles form on edge of cake and edge looks smooth and glossy or when underside is golden brown. Flip and brown other side. Place on a warming platter until ready to serve.

When another player in your foursome asks you to move and mark your ball on the putting green so that he has a clear roll to the cup, as a reminder to replace your ball to the original position hold your putter upside down with the clubhead in your hand. This could save costly penalty strokes in a tournament.

Smoothie

This nonfat drink is a perfect wakeup call at the breakfast table.

1 cup fresh strawberries
1 banana, peeled
1 8-oz. cup vanilla or lemon nonfat yogurt
1/2 cup nonfat milk

Put all ingredients in a blender; add several ice cubes; blend until smooth. Pour into 2 8-oz. glasses. Slurp your smoothie. Serves 2.

Guilt-Free Eggnog

4 cups skim milk
1 container egg beaters
1/2 cup sugar
2 egg whites
2 TBS. sugar
1 pkg. Equal
1 tsp. vanilla
1 tsp. Brandy or Rum flavoring

Beat 1/2 cup sugar into egg beaters. Stir in milk. Cook over medium heat until mixture coats spoon. Cool. Beat egg whites until soft peaks form. Add 2 TBS. sugar and Equal slowly. Thoroughly mix egg whites into custard mixture. Add flavorings. Chill.

Sausage Strata

8 slices white bread, crust removed, cubed
1 lb. sausage, cooked, crumbled, well drained
1/2 cup shredded Swiss cheese
1/2 cup grated sharp Cheddar cheese
1/2 cup fresh mushrooms
1 1/2 cups nonfat milk
3/4 cup light cream or more milk
5 slightly beaten eggs
1 tsp. prepared mustard
1 tsp. Worcestershire sauce
salt & pepper

Grease 13x9-inch pan. Arrange bread cubes to line bottom of dish. Spread cooked sausage over bread; spread cheese and mushrooms. Combine mustard with milk; add rest of milk, cream, eggs, seasonings and pour over ingredients in baking dish. Refrigerate overnight. Bake at 350º about 35 to 45 minutes or until firm. Cool just a minute before cutting into large squares. Serve with fruit and coffee cake for brunch.

"You can talk to a fade but a hook won't listen." Lee Trevino

Everybody's Favorite Coffee Cake

Cake Batter
2 sticks margarine or butter
2 cups sugar
2 eggs
1 tsp. vanilla
1 pint nonfat sour cream
2 cups flour
2 tsp. baking powder
1/4 tsp. salt

Put butter, sugar, eggs, vanilla and nonfat sour cream in a bowl and mix with an electric mixer. Fold in flour, baking powder, and salt with a spoon.

Topping
2/3-1 cup chopped walnuts
4 TBS. brown sugar
1 tsp. cinnamon

Mix all topping ingredients together.

Preheat oven to 350°. Spray Bundt pan with vegetable oil. Pour 1/2 cake batter into Bundt pan; layer with 1/2 of the topping mixture; repeat layering with 1/2 batter and 1/2 topping pushing topping into batter. Bake about 45-55 minutes. Do not overcook or it won't be moist. Turn out of Bundt pan immediately.

Murphy's Law of the Golf Swing: If it feels natural, you're doing it wrong.

Zucchini Bread

3 beaten eggs
1 cup oil
2 cups sugar
2 tsp. vanilla
2 cups shredded zucchini
1 8-oz. can crushed pineapple
3 cups flour
2 tsp. baking soda
1 tsp. salt
1 1/2 tsp. cinnamon
1/2 tsp. baking powder
3/4 tsp. nutmeg
1 cup chopped walnuts
1 cup currants

Beat eggs, oil, sugar and vanilla until foamy. Add zucchini and drained pineapple. Mix dry ingredients and add to mixture. Add walnuts and currants. Divide batter in 2 5x9-inch pans. Bake at 350º for 1 hour. Cool in pans 10 minutes. Turn on wire rack and cool thoroughly.

There are only 3 parts to a golf game. The power game, the short game and the mental game. There are only 2 parts to the golf swing, distance and direction.

Golfer's Overnight French Toast

2 TBS. corn syrup (dark or light)
1/2 cup butter
1 cup packed brown sugar
1 loaf white bread (crust removed)

5 eggs
1 1/2 cups milk
1 tsp. vanilla
1/4 tsp. salt

Combine syrup, butter, sugar; simmer until syrupy. Pour into 9x13-inch greased pan. Put bread over mixture, overlapping slices. Combine eggs, milk, vanilla and salt. Pour over bread. Cover and refrigerate overnight. Uncover and bake 45 minutes in a 350° oven. Cut and turn over onto plates. Serve hot. Serves 6-8.

Breakfast Sausage Casserole

1 lb. Jimmy Dean regular sausage, browned
1 clove garlic, minced
1 cup (8 oz.) grated extra sharp Cheddar
1/4 cup butter, melted
2 large eggs, well beaten
1 8-oz. can mild green chilies, seeded, chopped

1 cup grits
2 cups boiling water
1/2 tsp. salt
1/8 tsp. pepper
Tabasco

Brown sausage and drain on a paper towel. Sauté garlic with Tabasco; salt and pepper; set aside. Cook grits in 2 cups of boiling water. Mix sausage, grits and remaining ingredients and pour into well-buttered 9x13x2-inch baking dish; bake uncovered at 350° for about 1 hour. Serves 10.

French Omelet

Cheese, ham, and assorted sautéed vegetables can be added to this recipe for a variety of flavors.

2 eggs
1 TBS. water

1/8 tsp. salt
1 TBS. butter or margarine

Mix eggs, water and salt in a bowl. Put butter in a skillet and melt to coat bottom and sides. Put egg mixture in pan and cook at medium heat until eggs set, lifting once to let uncooked portion run behind set portion. When all is set, fold in thirds and place on warm plate. Serves 1.

Baked Apple Pecan Pancake

3/4 cup pancake mix
1/2 cup water
3 eggs
1/4 cup plus 1 TBS. sugar
1/2 cup butter or margarine

3 cups thinly sliced, peeled apples
1/4 cup chopped pecans
1/2 cup raisins
1 tsp. cinnamon

In a large bowl, combine pancake mix, water, eggs and 1 TBS. sugar. Mix well; set aside. Melt butter in a skillet over medium heat. Add apples and sauté until tender, stirring frequently. Remove skillet from heat. Spoon apples into ungreased pie plate. Sprinkle pecans and raisins over apples. Pour batter over fruit. In a small bowl, combine 1/4 cup sugar and cinnamon; sprinkle over batter. Loosely cover pie plate with foil and bake at 450° for 12-14 minutes or until pancake is puffed and sugar is melted. Loosen sides of pancake from pie plate; cool slightly. Cut pancake into wedges and serve. Serves 4-6.

Egg Strata

1 loaf torn bread, crust removed
3 cups milk
2 sliced tomatoes
8 eggs
1 cup Cheddar cheese

salt, pepper
1 tsp. dry mustard
1 pkg. sausage, cooked
1 sliced green pepper

Grease 9x12-inch casserole dish. Break bread into casserole. Discard crusts. Pour beaten liquid over bread. Arrange peppers, tomatoes, sausage and cheese on top. Chill overnight in refrigerator. Bake at 350° for 45 minutes.

Orange Waffles

1/2 cup pecans, lightly toasted
1 1/3 cups flour
2 TBS. sugar
4 tsp. baking powder
1/2 tsp. salt
2 tsp. freshly grated orange peel

2 large eggs
1/4 cup unsalted butter, melted, cooled
1 1/2 cups club soda
1 cup maple syrup

In a blender or food processor, grind pecans with flour, sugar, baking powder and salt until fine. Transfer to a large bowl; stir in orange peel. In a small bowl, whisk together eggs and butter. Add to flour mixture. Stir in club soda. Bake waffles in preheated waffle iron. Heat maple syrup and orange juice in microwave or small saucepan. Pass hot syrup to drizzle over hot waffles.

Doughnut Muffins

1/3 cup shortening
1 cup sugar
1 egg
1 1/2 cups flour
1 1/2 tsp. salt

1/2 tsp. nutmeg
1/2 cup milk
6 TBS. butter
1/2 cup sugar
1 tsp. cinnamon

Cream together shortening and sugar. Add egg and beat well. Add dry ingredients alternately with milk. Fill greased muffin pans 2/3 full. Bake at 350° for 20-30 minutes. Melt 6 TBS. butter. Roll muffins in butter then dip in mixture of 1/2 cup sugar and 1 tsp. cinnamon.

Nina's Granola

3 TBS. butter
1/4 cup brown sugar
1 tsp. vanilla
3 cups Quaker oats
1/4-1/2 cup oat bran
1/4-1/2 cup almonds
1/2-1 cup coconut, unsweetened

Melt butter and brown sugar together and stir. Add vanilla. Mix next 4 ingredients together and then stir into butter mixture to coat. Spread mixture onto a cookie sheet and bake for 20 minutes in a 350° oven. Refrigerate. Serve in a bowl with milk and fresh fruit.

Dutch Apple Pancake

This recipe is also good with fresh peaches.

6 TBS. butter
2 tsp. cinnamon
1/4 cup sugar
3 large Granny Smith apples, peeled, cored, sliced
4 eggs
1 cup flour
1 cup milk
1 1/2 TBS. powdered sugar

Preheat oven to 425º. In a 12-inch ovenproof frying pan, melt the butter over medium high heat. Stir in the cinnamon and sugar. Thinly slice the apples into the pan. Cook, stirring until the apples are translucent, approximately 5 minutes. Arrange the apples evenly in the pan and place uncovered in the oven for about 5 minutes while making the batter. In a blender, whirl the eggs and flour until smooth. Blend in the milk. Pour the batter evenly over the apples. Bake, uncovered, until the pancake is puffy and golden, about 15 minutes. Dust with powdered sugar and cut into wedges. Serve warm. Serves 6.

The mark of a champion is the ability to make the most of good luck and the best of bad.

Cathy's Cornbread

1 cup cornmeal
1 cup all purpose flour
1/3 cup granulated sugar
2 1/2 tsp. baking powder
1/4 tsp. salt

1 cup buttermilk
1 cup bacon, fried, diced
6 TBS. butter, melted
1 egg, slightly beaten

Preheat oven to 400°. Grease a 9-inch square baking pan. Stir dry ingredients together in a bowl. Stir in buttermilk, bacon, butter and egg and mix gently. Pour batter into the prepared pan, place in oven and bake for 25 minutes or until a knife inserted in the center comes out clean. Cut and serve with lots of butter and honey.

Cranberry Muffins

Notice the lowfat adjustments included in this recipe.

1 egg **or** 2 egg whites
1/2 cup millk **or** nonfat milk
1/4 cup salad oil **or** applesauce
1 1/2 cups all purpose flour

1/2 cup sugar
2 tsp. baking powder
1/2 tsp. salt
1 cup cranberries, cut in half

Heat oven to 400°. Grease bottoms of 12 medium muffin cups (2 3/4-inch in diameter). Beat egg, stir in milk and oil. Mix in remaining ingredients just until flour is moistened. Batter should be lumpy. Fill muffin cups 2/3 full. Bake 20-25 minutes or until golden brown. Immediately remove from pan.

Cranberry Scones

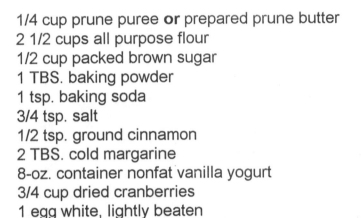

1/4 cup prune puree **or** prepared prune butter
2 1/2 cups all purpose flour
1/2 cup packed brown sugar
1 TBS. baking powder
1 tsp. baking soda
3/4 tsp. salt
1/2 tsp. ground cinnamon
2 TBS. cold margarine
8-oz. container nonfat vanilla yogurt
3/4 cup dried cranberries
1 egg white, lightly beaten
1 TBS. sugar

To puree prunes, combine 1 1/3 cups pitted prunes and 6 TBS. hot water in a blender. Blend until smooth. Preheat oven to 400º. Spray a baking sheet with cooking spray. Combine flour, brown sugar, baking powder, baking soda, salt and cinnamon. Cut in the 1/4 cup prune puree and margarine with pastry blender until coarse crumbs are formed. Mix in yogurt and stir in cranberries. Roll out to 3/4 inch thick. Cut out with biscuit cutter or floured glass. Arrange about 2 inches apart, brush with egg white and sprinkle with sugar. Bake about 15 minutes.

Practice makes perfect but practicing the wrong swing only grooves the wrong moves. Be sure to go and see your favorite golf instructor before you create a monster.

Renee's Blueberry Muffins

1 3/4 cups all purpose flour
1/3 cup sugar
2 1/2 tsp. baking powder
1/2 tsp. salt
1 cup fresh or thawed frozen blueberries (can use raisins or apples)
3/4 cup nonfat milk
1 egg
1/3 cup applesauce (or 1/3 cup melted butter if you like the fat)

In a large bowl, combine flour, sugar, baking powder and salt. Stir in blueberries. Add milk, egg and applesauce or butter. Mix just until dry ingredients are moistened. The batter will be lumpy. DO NOT OVERBEAT. Spoon batter into twelve 1/2-inch greased muffin cups. Bake at 400° for 25 minutes or until tops spring back when lightly touched. Serve warm and bring to your favorite foursome. Makes 12 muffins.

"Talent is only on loan, it's not given on a permanent basis."
Gary Player

Trary's Banana Bread

3 large overripe bananas
1 egg (or substitute egg beaters)
1/2 cup sugar
1 3/4 cups all purpose flour

3 TBS. butter or margarine (melted)
1 tsp. baking soda
1 tsp. salt

Preheat oven to 325°. Spray no-stick cooking spray in 9x5-inch loaf pan. Mash bananas in mixing bowl. Beat in sugar, egg, and butter. In a separate bowl, stir together flour, salt and baking soda. Stir dry ingredients into banana mixture until moistened. Pour batter into loaf pan. Bake 55-60 minutes or until loaf pulls away from sides of pan and a wooden toothpick inserted into center of loaf comes out clean. Makes one loaf.

Boston Brown Bread

2 cups graham flour
2 cups buttermilk
1 cup raisins
1/2 cup flour

1/2 cup molasses
2 tsp. baking soda
1 tsp. salt
2 1-lb. coffee cans

Grease 2 1-lb. coffee cans. Combine all ingredients and mix well. Fill cans 2/3 full; let stand 30 minutes. Preheat oven to 350°. Bake about 50 minutes. Let stand until cool. Can be foil wrapped and frozen.

Janusz's Huevos Rancheros de Baja

1/2 onion, chopped
1 dozen eggs
1 16-oz. jar Mild Ortega Salsa
1/4 cup milk

1/2 cup each grated Mozzarella
and Cheddar cheese
salt, pepper to taste

Sauté onion in a large pan. Whisk eggs, salt, pepper and milk together. Add mixture to onions in pan and scramble. When eggs are cooked, put salsa and cheese on top, cover and simmer until cheese is melted. Place on a platter and garnish with chilies and parsley or cilantro. Serves 6.

Croom's French Bread

This makes French bread but also makes a wonderful pizza dough. Just use nonfat cheese, Contadina pizza sauce and any vegetable you like.

2 1/2 cups warm water
1 pkg. dry yeast
2 TBS. sugar

1 TBS. salt
6-7 cups unbleached flour
herbs as desired

Mix water, yeast, sugar and salt and let it start, about 10 minutes. Stir in about 4-5 cups of flour; knead in remaining flour. Now place in a greased bowl and cover with greased plastic wrap. Put in a warm place and let rise about 1 hour. Push down and separate into pans or knots or shape into baguettes. Let it rise again. Bake at 375° for 10 minutes. Brush with water, lower temperature to 350° and bake for about 20 minutes or until bread shakes out of the pan. Makes 3 loaves.

Dilly Bread

2 TBS. yeast
1 TBS. sugar
1 cup warm water
4 cups flour
2 TBS. sugar
1/2 TBS. baking soda
1 envelope onion soup mix
1 cup large curd Cottage cheese
1 cup sour cream
2 eggs, lightly beaten
4 tsp. each dill seed & dill weed

Stir yeast and sugar into warm water; let stand until bubbles form. Combine flour, sugar and baking soda and sift; add yeast mix; add remaining ingredients and blend until smooth. Knead about 5 minutes adding enough flour for stiff dough. Put dough in buttered bowl, turn over and let rise 1 1/2 hours. Punch down, knead 3-4 minutes, put in bread pans (half full). Let rise 1 hour. Brush top with 1 egg and 1 TBS. milk beaten together. Bake in preheated 375º oven or until loaves sound hollow when tapped, turn out on rack, brush tops with butter. Let cool.

"I just try to put it on the fairway, then the green and not threeputt."
Peter Thomson

Tee Off
—
Appetizers

Tee Off - Appetizers

Shrimp & Swiss Cheese Canapé

1 can shrimp, drained, broken
1/2 tsp. curry powder or to taste
1/2 tsp. chopped fresh dill
1/2 lb. Swiss cheese, grated

1 tsp. onion juice
1/3 cup mayonnaise, lowfat or regular
dash of Tabasco

Mix all ingredients together, adding more mayonnaise if necessary for spreading consistency. Best if refrigerated a few hours or overnight. Spread on crackers or French bread slices and put under broiler until they just start to brown.

Esther's Zesty Seafood Spread

1 8-oz. pkg. lowfat cream cheese, softened
1/4 cup Heinz Chili Sauce
1 tsp. lemon juice
1/4-1/2 tsp. hot pepper sauce
1 cup (1/2 lb.) chopped cooked shrimp and crab
4 sliced green onions, including some tops
1/4 cup finely chopped red Bell pepper
1/4 cup finely chopped celery
crackers, bagel chips, pita crisps

In a bowl thoroughly combine cream cheese, chili sauce, lemon juice and hot pepper sauce. Stir in seafood, onions, Bell pepper and celery until well blended. Transfer to serving bowl. Serve with crackers, bagel chips or pita crisps.

Burritos Canapés

These tasty rollups can be made ahead for the freezer. To freeze, place un-cut tortilla rolls in a plastic bag and save for something quick to serve after a perfect day on the course, or for unexpected guests.

10 8" flour tortillas
1 8-oz. carton sour cream
1 8-oz. pkg. cream cheese, softened
1-2 cloves garlic, minced
3 green onions, chopped
1 4-oz. can diced green chilies
salt
pepper
picante sauce

Mix sour cream, cream cheese, garlic, onions, and chilies. Salt and pepper to taste. Spread on tortillas and roll up. Chill for 1 hour before slicing into 1-inch rounds. Secure with cocktail picks. Serve with picante sauce for dipping.

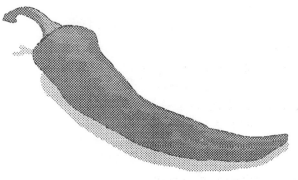

 Trust your swing. Learn one basic shot that you can hit under pressure and stick with it.

Bruschetta

Be sure to buy tomatoes a few days early and place in a brown paper bag to ripen. A very easy starter, you'll get raves.

7-8 ripe, Roma tomatoes, chopped
3-5 cloves garlic, chopped
fresh basil
1/4 cup olive oil
2 TBS. balsamic vinegar
light cream cheese
Gorgonzola cheese
baguette of French bread
salt
pepper

Cut, seed, and chop ripe Roma tomatoes and place in a medium size bowl. Peel and chop 3-5 cloves of fresh garlic. Tear 10 leaves of fresh basil into small pieces. Add 2 TBS. of balsamic vinegar and 1/4 cup of olive oil to tomato mixture. Salt and pepper to taste.

Mix equal amounts of light cream cheese and Gorgonzola cheese together in a separate bowl.

Slice baguette into 1/2 inch rounds. Put on cookie sheet and place under the broiler until golden brown on both sides. Watch closely to keep from burning.

Serve cheese mixture as a spread on toast rounds and top with tomato mixture.

Teriyaki Style Shrimp

This recipe adds spice and flavor to the ordinary shrimp.

1/2 cup soy sauce
1/2 cup olive oil
1/2 cup Sherry
2 TBS. lemon juice
1/2 tsp. garlic salt
1/2 tsp. ground ginger
1/4 tsp. ground rosemary
1/4 tsp. thyme
1/4 tsp. oregano
1/4 tsp. marjoram
2 lbs. shrimp, shelled & veined
fresh dill or parsley for garnish

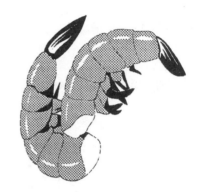

Mix soy, oil, Sherry, lemon juice, garlic salt, ginger, rosemary, thyme, oregano and marjoram. Pour over shrimp. Put in refrigerator and let stand 1-2 hours. Remove shrimp from marinade and broil 5-7 minutes. Arrange on a serving plate and garnish with lemons and fresh dill or parsley. Makes 12 to 14 servings.

When making a golf swing, stay grounded and balanced. You can't shoot a cannon from a canoe.

Crab Dip

A cheesy crab dip that's easy and perfect for a party.

8 oz. cream cheese
1 TBS. minced shallots
1/2 tsp. horseradish

1/2 tsp. salt & pepper
1 6-oz. can Alaskan crabmeat
crackers

Mix and bake at 375° for 20 minutes. Serve with crackers.

Sandi's Crab Mold

1 pkg. gelatin
3 TBS. cold water
1 can cream of mushroom soup
6-8 oz. cream cheese
1 cup celery, diced
1 small onion, minced
1 7 1/2-oz. can crabmeat or fresh cracked crab
3/4 cup mayonnaise
crackers

Mix gelatin and water in saucepan; add cream of mushroom soup and the rest of ingredients except mayonnaise. Heat until smooth but do not boil. Remove from heat and add mayonnaise; pour into mold and refrigerate until firm. Unmold onto serving plate and serve with crackers.

Shrimp In Dijon Vinaigrette

For a tangy flavored shrimp this recipe will fill the bill.

3 lbs. shrimp
1/2 cup fresh parsley, finely chopped
1/2 cup shallots, chopped
1/2 cup tarragon vinegar
1/2 cup white wine vinegar
1 cup olive oil

8 TBS. Dijon mustard
4 tsp. red pepper flakes
2 tsp. salt
fresh ground pepper
1 TBS. lemon juice

Place all ingredients except shrimp in a large bowl. Stir mixture and adjust seasoning to taste. Add shrimp and toss. Cover with plastic wrap and marinate in refrigerator for 2 hours. Drain before serving.

Crabmeat On Muffins

This recipe can be made as an hors d'oeuvre or a light supper or lunch.

4 sour dough muffins, split, toasted
2 hard boiled eggs, chopped
1 can crabmeat (or fresh)
1/4 cup chopped green onions

1/2 cup chopped celery
1/2 cup grated Cheddar cheese
pinch of salt, pepper and oregano
1/4 cup light mayonnaise

Blend ingredients except muffins. Mound on warm toasted muffins and heat under broiler. If doing for hors d'oeuvres, spread mixture on small bread rounds, put on cookie sheet and place under broiler until bubbly.

Parmesan Parsley Pizza

A light bread pizza, cut into small pieces and passed with cocktails. Make dough in bread maker before going to the golf course. It will rise and will be ready to form into pizza shape when you return.

Bread Dough
7/8 cup water
2 cups bread flour
1 tsp. salt

1 TBS. dried milk
1 TBS. sugar
1 1/2 tsp. yeast

Pizza
1 recipe bread dough
3 cloves garlic (finely chopped)
3 TBS. olive oil
3 oz. grated Mozzarella cheese

3 oz. grated Fontina cheese
2 bunches whole Italian parsley
6 oz. shaved chunk Reggiano Parmesan

To make pizza: Combine garlic and olive oil and let stand 30 minutes. Reserve 1/4 of mixture for vinaigrette. Do not let sit overnight. Pick parsley leaves from stems and discard stems. Wash leaves and spin dry. Roll dough into desired shape on floured surface. It should be about 1/4 inch thick. Transfer to well-floured pizza peel. Brush dough to within 1/2 inch of edge with garlic oil. Sprinkle combined cheese over dough. Transfer dough from peel to heated brick. Bake at 500° for 10 minutes or until golden and crisp. Toss parsley with vinaigrette and season with salt and pepper. Spread on top of baked pizza. Shave Parmesan on top. Serve immediately.

Vinaigrette
3 TBS. extra virgin olive oil
3 TBS. olive oil

1 1/2 TBS. freshly squeezed lemon juice
1 1/2 TBS. champagne vinegar
1/4 garlic mixture from pizza recipe

Combine both olive oils, add lemon juice and champagne vinegar whisking together. Add 1/4 of reserved garlic mixture. Season with salt and pepper.

Hot Sherry Crab Dip

3 8-oz. pkgs. cream cheese
1/2 cup mayonnaise
2 scant tsp. prepared mustard
dash of garlic salt
2 tsp. confectioners sugar
1 tsp. onion juice
1/2 -1 tsp. seasoned salt
1/3-2/3 cup Sauterne wine or Sherry
1 lb. lump fresh crabmeat or 3 cans good quality crabmeat or 3 6-oz. pkgs. frozen crabmeat

In top of double boiler, melt cream cheese until softened. Add remaining ingredients except crab. Stir until smooth. Fold in crab. Heat thoroughly. Serve very hot in a chafing dish or on a hot tray with warmed crackers or melba toast. If made ahead, reheat in 350º oven until hot. Yields 15 to 20 servings.

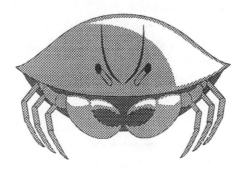

 Teeing off is like riding in a taxi, you can't rush the driver.

Lori West's
Italian Stuffed Artichokes

Contributed by
Lori West
LPGA Professional

4 plump, ripe artichokes
1 cup Progresso Italian style seasoned bread crumbs
1 cup Parmesan cheese, freshly grated
4 cloves garlic, minced
olive oil

Clean and trim artichokes; rinse them thoroughly, turn upside down and push on them to open up the leaves; if the tips of the leaves are prickly, cut off the tips with scissors; cut off the stems at the base of the artichokes, leaving a flat surface. (If you like, you can peel the stems, mince them and add them to the stuffing-they're delicious but they might turn your fingers a little black.) In a large bowl mix the bread crumbs, grated cheese, garlic, and minced stems. Stuff each artichoke, usually about 1/2 cup of mix per artichoke (use your judgment and remember-no skimping, they're Italian artichokes). Place stuffed artichokes in a large steamer basket and drizzle the tops with olive oil to moisten the stuffing. Cover and steam for 45 minutes or until a leaf pulls out easily. If you are preparing these ahead of time, you can warm the pre-cooked artichokes in a baking pan; cover with foil, and bake at 350° for about 15 minutes. If you like them crispy, take the foil off for the last 5 minutes. Serve as an appetizer, or as a side dish with your favorite pasta. If one artichoke is too much for one person, you can cut the finished product into halves. Mangia!

"Let 'em hang, your arms that is. After you set up, let your arms relax and hang down, then grip the club. You'll notice that there will be less tension in your setup, and therefore, less tension in your swing."
Lori West

Reuben Dip Canapé

A great dish that can be made ahead and frozen.

1 lb. can sauerkraut, drained
1/2 lb. chopped corned beef **or** 1 12-oz. can
2 tsp. Dijon mustard
1/2 cup mayonnaise

Mix all ingredients and put in greased casserole. Bake at 400° for 20 minutes. Bake longer if dish has been refrigerated. Serve with crackers or thin rye bread.

Roasted Portobello Mushrooms with Fontina Cheese

2 TBS. olive oil
1 TBS. chopped fresh basil
1 TBS. chopped fresh parsley
2 garlic cloves, minced
4 4-5-inch diameter Portobello mushrooms, stems removed
8 oz. Fontina cheese, cut in 3x1/2x1/2-inch strips
4 slices bread from crusty round loaf, lightly toasted

Mix first 4 ingredients in bowl. Place mushrooms, stem side up, on heavy large baking sheet. Brush with oil mixture. Season with salt and pepper. Broil mushrooms until just cooked through, about 3 minutes. Place on work surface. Set oven temperature at 450°. Cut each mushroom crosswise in 1/2-inch strips. Alternate mushroom strips and cheese strips atop each bread slice. Place bread on baking sheet. Bake until cheese melts, about 5 minutes.

Cajun Chicken Wings

24 whole chicken wings (about 4 lbs.)
1 TBS. cayenne pepper
2 TBS. paprika
2 TBS. garlic powder
1 TBS. dried oregano
1 TBS. dried thyme leaves
1 TBS. onion powder
1 TBS. salt
1/2 tsp. freshly ground white pepper
1/2 tsp. freshly ground black pepper
1/4 cup olive oil

Rinse chicken with cold water and pat dry. Cut off and discard pointed tip of each wing and halve wings at the main joint. In a food processor or blender, combine cayenne, paprika, garlic powder, oregano, thyme, onion powder, salt, white pepper and black pepper. Process until well blended. With machine on, slowly pour in oil and process until a thick paste forms. In a large bowl, combine chicken wings and spice paste. Toss until wings are well coated. Cover and refrigerate overnight. Preheat broiler. Arrange wings on broiler pan about 4 inches from heat. Broil, turning once until nicely browned outside and cooked through, about 20 minutes. Serve warm or at room temperature. Makes 48.

 To intentionally produce a draw or a fade, align your body in the direction you want the ball to start and align your clubface in the direction you want the ball to finish.

Artichoke Dip

This dip can also be used to fill mushroom caps. For an extra zip add some Ortega chilies or Tabasco.

1 can artichoke hearts in water, chopped
3/4 cup mayonnaise
3/4 cup Parmesan cheese, grated
2 dashes of garlic salt

Drain, squeeze, then chop artichoke. Mix all ingredients. Place in oven proof dish. Heat at 350° for 15-20 minutes until bubbly. Serve with tortilla chips or crackers.

Pears Wrapped in Arugula & Prosciutto

Pears take the place of the usual melon in this recipe when melons are not in season.

12 thin slices of prosciutto (about 1/3 lb.)
12 leaves arugula, thick stem removed; more for garnish
2 pears, cored and cut in 6 wedges each

Lay a piece of prosciutto on a flat surface and put an arugula leaf down the center. Put a pear wedge in the center of the arugula. Drape each end of the prosciutto over the pear. Arrange the pears, sticking outward, on a platter in a circular spoke pattern, with arugula or fresh herbs in the center. Can be made 2 hours ahead, covered with plastic wrap, and refrigerated.

Brie with Sun Dried Tomatoes

1 lb. Brie, chilled
2 TBS. minced fresh parsley
2 TBS. fresh grated Parmesan
4 sun dried tomatoes (packed in oil)
1 tsp. dried basil
1 TBS. olive oil
6 garlic cloves, minced and mashed to a paste
crackers

Remove rind from Brie. Put on serving plate. In a small bowl, combine parsley, Parmesan, tomatoes, garlic, basil, and oil. Spread mixture over Brie and let stand 1 hour before serving. Serve with crackers. Serves 6.

Wonton Shells for Hors d'Oeuvres

1 pkg. wonton wrappers
cooking spray
filling, tuna salad, chicken salad, etc.

Preheat oven to 350º. Trim wonton wrappers to 2-inch squares. Coat 2 mini-muffin tins with cooking spray and press a wonton square into each cup. Lightly coat squares with cooking spray and bake for about 7 minutes or until lightly browned. Let cool in the pan. The shells can be stored in an airtight container at room temperature for up to a week. Yields 5 dozen.

Olive or Sausage Balls

2 sticks margarine, softened at room temperature
2 3-oz. pkgs. cream cheese, softened
2 cups sifted flour
1 7-oz. jar Spanish olives **or** 1 pkg. pre-cooked smoked sausage links, cut into bite-sized pieces

Using a large fork or electric mixer, blend margarine and cream cheese; add flour and blend to a consistency of cookie dough. Drain the olives and pat dry with a paper towel. Pinch off a small amount of the dough and wrap it around an olive or sausage bite. Place on a plate and freeze if desired. Bake at 400° until brown on the bottom, about 20 minutes. If frozen, bake a little longer. Dough wraps 60-70 pieces.

Corn Chip Dip

This favorite can be served in a chafing dish to keep it piping hot.

1 8-oz. pkg. cream cheese (room temperature)
1 can Hormel Chili Without Beans
1 8-oz. jar picante salsa
8 oz. shredded Cheddar cheese

In a 9-inch round microwave proof dish spread cream cheese and layer remaining ingredients in order given. Microwave on high until hot, 4-6 minutes. Serve with corn chips.

Rosemary-Olive Focaccia

Prepared frozen bread dough or dough prepared in a bread machine makes this recipe simple. Serving the focaccia with an infused oil makes it even tastier.

1 pound bread dough
3 TBS. olive oil
1 TBS. minced fresh rosemary **or** 1 tsp. dried
3/4 cup grated Parmesan cheese
6 Kalamata olives
4 oil-packed sun-dried tomatoes
2 large cloves garlic
pepper

Preheat oven to 450°. Place bread dough in bowl. Add 1 TBS. oil and minced rosemary. Season generously with pepper. Knead dough until ingredients are combined. Roll dough out on floured surface. Transfer to baking sheet. Rub with 1 TBS. olive oil. Sprinkle 1/2 cup cheese over; press generously into dough. Bake until bread is almost cooked through and cheese begins to brown, about 12 minutes. Arrange olives, sun-dried tomatoes and garlic atop bread. Sprinkle remaining cheese over to cover lightly. Drizzle remaining oil over. Continue baking 5 minutes.
Cut and serve.

Murphy's Law of the New Golf Club: A demo club that will produce a perfect golf swing today will produce your normal swing as soon as the price tag is removed tomorrow.

Salmon Mousse

1 envelope plain gelatin
1/4 cup canned salmon juice
1/4 cup boiling water
1/2 small onion, minced
2 TBS. lemon juice
1/2 cup mayonnaise
1 TBS. horseradish
2 tsps. Worcestershire
2 drops Tabasco
1/4 tsp. paprika
1 tsp. dill weed
1 lb. can red salmon, drained & boned

Dissolve gelatin in 1/4 cup of cold salmon juice, then add the 1/4 cup of boiling water and blend well in food processor. Add all other ingredients in processor and mix until smooth. Use 1 quart (shallow) mold that has been sprayed with Pam. Spread mixture into mold, cover with plastic wrap and put into refrigerator until jelled. Remove onto serving plate, garnish with parsley and serve with crackers. Serves 15.

When hitting into the wind, tee it low and swing slow.

Pesto Cheese Mold Torta

For a quick version of this recipe, substitute prepared pesto from the grocer. Also a layer of prepared sun-dried tomato spread can be used for more color and an additional flavor.

1 cup lowfat Ricotta cheese
4 oz. light cream cheese
1/4 tsp. salt
1/8 tsp. pepper
pesto filling
fresh basil sprigs
1/4 cup pine nuts
thin baguette slices
crisp raw vegetables
cheese cloth for mold

With mixer, beat Ricotta and cream cheese until well blended. Add salt and pepper. If using prepared pesto sauce, squeeze all the excess oil from the mixture (too much oil will bleed into the cream cheese layers). Toast pine nuts in a pan over low heat. Shake pan to keep from burning. Mix toasted pine nuts into the pesto. Smoothly line a fancy mold with a double layer of moistened cheese cloth. With a spoon, press 1/4 of cheese into mold. Press 1/3 pesto onto cheese. Repeat, finishing with cheese. Fold cloth over; cover airtight and chill at least 2 hours. Fold back cloth and invert torta onto plate. Garnish with basil sprig. Spread on bread or toast or serve with vegetables.

Pesto Filling
If you're not using a prepared pesto prepare your filling according to the following directions. In a blender or processor, whirl 2 1/2 cups lightly packed fresh basil leaves, 1 cup (5 oz.) freshly grated Parmesan, 1 TBS. olive oil and 1-2 TBS. water to make smooth paste. Stir in 1/4 cup pine nuts and season with salt to taste.

Jane's Cheddar Biscuits

5 cups flour
2 TBS. baking powder
4 TBS. sugar
1/2 tsp. salt
1 cup heavy cream **or** half and half
1 cup buttermilk
1/2 lb. butter, melted
1 cup grated Cheddar cheese
2 TBS. chopped chives

Preheat oven to 375º. Sift together flour, baking powder, sugar and salt. In a separate bowl mix heavy cream, buttermilk and melted butter. Combine liquid ingredients with dry. Mix with a wooden spoon until dough pulls together but is still crumbly. Stir in grated cheese and chives. On a floured surface, roll dough to 1-inch thickness and cut in 1 1/2-inch rounds. Bake on a baking sheet covered with parchment paper for about 15-20 minutes or until tops are golden brown. Serve plain or split in half and stuff with ham, chutney or your choice of filling. Very rich, very good, and worth the fat content. Just eat a couple? Makes approximately 6 dozen.

When teeing off with the wind behind, tee it high and let it fly.

Atherton's Gravlax

1 King or Silver salmon filet, skinned and all bones removed with needlenose pliers. To eliminate any worry about parasites because the fish is uncooked, freeze the filet for 48 hours and then defrost.

1/2 cup kosher salt
1 tsp. dill seed
1 white onion, minced
1/2 bunch fresh dill, optional

1/2 cup sugar
1 TBS. black peppercorns
juice from 1 lemon
cream cheese, capers, crackers or bread rounds

Grind dill seeds and peppercorns to medium coarse. Mix the kosher salt and the sugar. Add the lemon juice to the minced onion. Chop the fresh dill. In a glass baking dish - NOT METAL- spread about 1/3 cup of the salt and sugar mix. Rub the dill and pepper mixture into both sides of the salmon. Place salmon into baking dish on top of the salt and sugar mixture. Cover the salmon with the remaining salt and sugar mix. Sprinkle the fresh dill on top. Here's where you can get creative. Use 1/2 of the onion and lemon mix combined with about 1-2 TBS. white wine and/or 1 TBS. low sodium soy sauce and sprinkle that over the top, or try some other flavors. Cover tightly with plastic wrap and place in the refrigerator with one end slightly elevated. About 3-4 times during the next 18 to 24 hours, drain the liquid which has accumulated; refrigerate again reversing the elevated end. The length of time to marinate the salmon depends upon the thickness of the filet. When ready, rinse most of the salt and sugar mixture off but try to keep as much dill and pepper mix on as possible. Pat dry and rub in a small amount of vegetable oil to coat. Slice very thin and serve with cream cheese, capers, the remaining onion and lemon mixture and crackers or small bread rounds.

Caviar Mousse

1 pkg. Knox gelatin
2 TBS. lemon juice
2 TBS. water
1 tsp. Worcestershire sauce
6 hard boiled eggs, finely chopped
1/2 cup light mayonnaise
1/2 cup nonfat sour cream
onion powder
large jar of black caviar

Spray pie plate lightly with vegetable oil. Mix eggs, mayonnaise, sour cream, and onion powder. Heat gelatin, lemon juice, water and Worcester-shire sauce together, stirring, less than a minute. Quickly pour into egg mixture, stir well and pour total mixture into pie plate. Jell in refrigerator (about an hour). Flip out small side up on large serving tray. Pat juice out of caviar and spread over top just before serving. Decorate with twisted lemon rind and parsley or green onions. Place crackers in ring around outside of mousse.

"If you've got to remind yourself to concentrate during competition, you've got no chance to concentrate." Bobby Nichols

Spicy Holiday Nuts

3 TBS. butter
1 TBS. finely chopped orange zest
2 tsp. finely chopped lemon zest
2 tsp. ground cinnamon
1 1/2 tsp. ground coriander
1 1/4 tsp. ground mace
1/4 tsp. cayenne pepper
2 TBS. plus 3 tsp. brown sugar
1/4 tsp. salt
1/2 lb. (about 2 1/2 cups) pecan halves
1/2 lb. (about 1 1/2 cups) blanched almonds

Heat the oven to 300º. In a large saucepan, melt the butter over medium-low heat. Add the orange and lemon zests, cinnamon, coriander, mace, cayenne, brown sugar, and salt. Combine until the mixture is bubbly and well blended. Add the nuts and stir to coat them evenly. Transfer the nut mixture to a baking sheet, spread it evenly, and bake for 25 minutes, stirring every 5-7 minutes. For crispier nuts, increase the cooking time to 35-40 minutes. Do not increase the heat or the nuts may burn. Yields 4 cups.

Murphy's Law of the Course: There is never anyone around to see your 260-yard drive. There is always a crowd to observe your shank.

Brie Torte

1 wheel (14 oz.) **or** 2 wheels (8 oz.) Brie
1/2 cup butter or margarine, softened
1 large clove garlic, pressed
1/3 cup finely chopped walnuts
1/3 cup finely chopped ripe olives
2 TBS. chopped fresh basil
assorted crackers

Place Brie in freezer 1/2 hour until very firm. Carefully cut into halves horizontally; set aside. Cream butter and garlic in small bowl. Mix in walnuts, olives and basil until blended. Spread evenly on cut side of 1 of the Brie halves. Top with the other Brie half, cut side down. Press together lightly. Wrap in plastic and refrigerate. Bring to room temperature before serving. Serve with assorted crackers.

 Big tournament nerves? You should be glad, it's a symptom of a real competitive fire inside you.

Southwestern Cheesecake

Crust
1 cup finely crushed tortilla chips
3 TBS. melted margarine

Heat oven to 325°. Mix chips and margarine in a small bowl; press onto bottom of a 9-inch springform pan. Bake 15 minutes.

Filling
2 8-oz. pkgs. cream cheese, softened
2 eggs
8 oz. shredded Cheddar cheese
1 4-oz. can chopped green chilies, drained **or** chopped jalapeño peppers

Beat cream cheese and eggs in large mixing bowl at medium speed with electric mixer until well blended. Mix in cheese and chilies; pour over crust. Bake 30 minutes.

Topping
1 cup sour cream
1/2 cup sliced green onions
1/3 cup chopped tomatoes
1/4 cup sliced pitted ripe olives

Spread sour cream over cheesecake. Loosen cake from rim of pan; cool before removing rim of pan. Refrigerate several hours. Top with remaining ingredients, starting with olives in the center, then tomatoes and onions placed in concentric circles. Serve with firm, large tortilla chips or crackers.

Down The Fairway

Entrées

Down The Fairway - Entrées

Duffy's Garlic Chicken

3 whole chicken breasts, halved, skinned and boned
1/2 tsp. salt
1/4 tsp. freshly ground pepper
4 1/2 TBS. Dijon mustard
3 1/2 TBS. butter
8 cloves garlic, finely chopped
1/2 cup chicken stock

1 16-oz. pkg. bow-tie pasta
1 1/2 TBS. butter
2 TBS. finely chopped parsley
1 1/2 tsp. finely chopped fresh basil
1 cup heavy cream
1 tsp. salt
1/4 tsp. freshly ground pepper

Put chicken breasts between plastic wrap and pound to a 3/8-inch thickness. Lightly salt and pepper chicken. Coat chicken with mustard and set aside for 10 minutes. Preheat oven to 350°. In a large skillet, over medium-high heat, melt 2 1/2 TBS. butter. Pan must be large enough to accommodate chicken without crowding. You may have to cook chicken in two batches. Quickly brown chicken on both sides. Remove pan from heat and transfer chicken to an oven-proof platter. Place in oven for approximately 10 minutes, or until chicken is done. In skillet, melt 1 TBS. butter over medium heat. Sauté garlic about 2 minutes; do not allow to brown. Add stock and simmer until liquid reduces by half. In a large pot, cook pasta al dente, according to package directions; drain in colander. While pasta is draining melt 1 1/2 TBS. butter in pot. Add pasta, 1 1/2 TBS. parsley and basil to pot. Cover with lid to keep warm. While pasta is cooking add cream, remaining parsley, salt and pepper to reduced stock. Stirring frequently simmer to reduce until sauce coats the back of a spoon. Transfer pasta to a warm platter and sprinkle with Parmesan. Place chicken on top of pasta and spoon garlic sauce over chicken.

 Suggested Wines: Medium-rich Chardonnay or Pinot Blanc.

George Archer's Really Wild Quail

Contributed by
George Archer
PGA Professional

One of the greatest displays of putting in a tournament came from George Archer when in a 72-hole tournament he took only 94 putts. The figure was 5 under the PGA tournament record.

quail
canned milk
flour
salt
pepper
lemon salt
canola oil

Clean birds; pluck all feathers; cut off wings and legs; split breasts. Soak cleaned birds in canned milk to cover, about 1 hour. Partially fill a small brown bag with flour, salt, pepper and lemon salt. Shake with birds inside until coated. Heat canola oil in a heavy pan until temperature is approximately 350°. Drop in floured birds and cook until they float to the top. Remove and drain on paper towels. To keep warm, put between layers of paper towels and put in oven set only to warm.

George and Donna Archer love this one and vow that "the quail tastes just like alligator meat!" Thought for the day. "When you eat game, be cautious about biting into shotgun BB's!" George Archer

 Suggested Wine: Medium-bodied Chardonnay.

Chicken with Herbs & Spices

4 chickens, 2 1/2 lbs. each, quartered
1 head garlic, peeled and finely pureed
1/4 cup dried oregano
coarse salt and freshly ground black pepper to taste
1/2 cup red wine vinegar
1/2 cup olive oil
1 cup pitted prunes
1/2 cup pitted Spanish green olives
1/2 cup capers with a bit of juice
6 bay leaves
1 cup brown sugar
1 cup white wine
1/4 cup Italian parsley **or** fresh cilantro, finely chopped

In a large bowl combine chicken quarters, garlic, oregano, pepper and
coarse salt to taste, vinegar, olive oil, prunes, olives, capers and juice, and
bay leaves. Cover and let marinate, refrigerated, overnight. Preheat oven to
350°. Arrange chicken in a single layer in one or two large, shallow baking
pans and spoon marinade over it evenly. Sprinkle chicken pieces with
brown sugar and pour white wine around them. Bake for 50 minutes to
1 hour, basting frequently with pan juices. Chicken is done when thigh
pieces, pricked with a fork at their thickest, yield clear yellow juice. With a
slotted spoon transfer chicken, prunes, olives and capers to a serving platter. Moisten with a few spoonfuls of pan juices and sprinkle generously with
parsley or cilantro. Pass remaining pan juices in a sauceboat.
Serves 10.

Chicken Pie & Onion Biscuits

1/2 large onion, chopped, divided in half
3 carrots, sliced
3 stalks celery, diced
1/2 green or red Bell pepper, diced
1/2 cup frozen peas
2 boneless skinless chicken breasts **or**
1 cup leftover roast chicken, diced

6 oz. mushrooms
2 TBS. flour
1/2 tsp. salt
1/4 tsp. pepper
1 14 1/2-oz. can chicken broth
2 TBS. butter

Par boil carrots in water until tender (10-20 minutes). Sauté chicken breasts in 1 TBS. butter until done. Remove from pan and dice. Add 1 TBS. butter and sauté peppers, celery and one half the onions until translucent and tender. Add mushrooms and sauté until tender. Add flour, salt and pepper and continue cooking about 2 minutes. Add chicken broth, diced chicken, carrots and peas. Simmer slowly about 5 minutes until thickened. Place in casserole. Prepare biscuits.

Biscuits
1 1/2 cups sifted flour
2 3/4 tsp. baking powder
1/2 tsp. salt

4 TBS. plus 1 tsp. butter
2/3 cup milk
reserved onions

Sauté reserved onions in 1 tsp. butter until lightly browned. Cut 4 TBS. butter into flour, baking powder and salt using pastry blender, food processor or fork. Mixture should have texture like cornmeal. Add milk and mix lightly. Knead lightly on floured surface. Pat out about 1/2-inch thick layer and cut into 2-inch rounds. Arrange on top of chicken mixture and bake in 450° oven 15-20 minutes until lightly browned. Serve immediately.

 Suggested Wines: A light red such as a Gamay Beaujolais or Cotes Du Rhone.

Schafer's Chicken Casserole

8 cups cooked chicken (2 whole)
1 small pkg. Pepperidge Farm stuffing
3 cups mayonnaise
2 cans water chestnuts, sliced
2 cans mushrooms, sliced
1/3 cup milk
1/3 cup Sherry

2 cups celery, chopped
1 stick butter
2 cups chopped onion
Parmesan cheese
paprika

Sauté onions and celery in butter but leave crunchy. Add chicken and all other ingredients except Parmesan and paprika. Place in a 3-quart casserole dish. Sprinkle top with Parmesan cheese, paprika and a little stuffing. Bake in a 350° oven for 45 minutes until hot throughout. Serves 12.

Gayle's Mexican Style Chicken Kiev

This dish is great when served with a fresh tomato salsa and spicy bread sticks.

8 boneless chicken breast halves
1 7-oz. can diced green chilies
4 oz. Monterey Jack cheese, cut into 8 strips
1/2 cup fine dry bread crumbs
1/4 cup Parmesan cheese
1 TBS. chili powder
1/2 tsp. salt
1/4 tsp. cumin
1/4 tsp. black pepper
butter, melted

Pound chicken to about 1/4-inch thickness. Put 2 TBS. chilies and 1 Jack cheese strip in center of each chicken piece. Roll up and tuck ends under. Combine bread crumbs, Parmesan cheese, chili powder, salt, cumin and pepper. Dip each stuffed chicken breast in shallow bowl containing 6 TBS. melted butter and roll in crumb mixture. Place chicken rolls, seam side down in oblong baking dish and drizzle with a little melted butter. Cover and chill 4 hours or overnight. Bake uncovered at 400° for 1/2 hour or until done. Serves 8.

 Suggested Wines: Gamay Beaujolais or a light Pinot Noir.

Cornish Hens with Orange Glaze

4 (1 1/2-2 lb.) Cornish hens
1/2 tsp. salt
1/2 tsp. dried whole basil
1/2 tsp. dried whole tarragon
1/2 tsp. dried whole thyme
1/2 tsp. ground savory
1/8 tsp. pepper
1/4 cup butter or margarine, melted
1/4 cup orange marmalade
watercress
peeled orange slices

Remove giblets from hens. Rinse hens with cold water and pat dry. Combine seasonings, stirring well. Sprinkle cavities with half of seasonings and close cavities. Secure with wooden picks, truss. Brush skin with butter and sprinkle with remaining seasonings.

Place hens, breast side up, on a rack in a shallow roasting pan. Pour water into pan to cover bottom (about 1/8 inch deep). Place in upper half of oven, and bake at 325° for 45 minutes.

Brush hens with butter and spoon 1 TBS. marmalade on each breast. Bake an additional 35 to 45 minutes or until juices run clear when thigh is pierced with a fork. Garnish hens with watercress and orange slices.

Always play the correct mental tape. If you see the shot in your mind's eye, your muscles will do their best to make it happen.

Sour Cream Chicken Enchiladas

4 cups sour cream
2 cups cooked and flaked chicken breasts, packed tightly
1/2 lb. fresh mushrooms, chopped
1 4-oz. can chopped green chilies, drained (use 2 cans for spicier dish)
1 med. onion, chopped
1 tsp. chili powder
1/2 tsp. salt
1 clove garlic, mashed
1/4 tsp. pepper
8 flour tortillas
2 cups shredded Cheddar cheese
green chili salsa
guacamole

In a 9 x 13 baking dish, spread 1 1/4 cups sour cream. Set aside. Mix 1/2 cup sour cream with other ingredients (except Cheddar cheese, flour tortillas, salsa and guacamole). Divide mixture and put some on each tortilla. Roll each tortilla and place seam side down in baking dish on top of sour cream. Cover with remaining sour cream, sprinkle with Cheddar cheese. Bake at 450° for 15 to 20 minutes or until heated and cheese melts. Serve with side of green chili salsa and guacamole.

 Suggested Wine: Gewurztraminer.

Barb's Turkey Medallions

1 1/4 to 1 1/2 lbs. turkey tenderloins
1 med. onion, thinly sliced
1 stalk celery with leaves, thinly sliced
3 peppercorns
1/2 tsp. salt
1 bay leaf

Place tenderloins in large skillet. Add onions, celery, peppercorns, salt and bay leaf with enough water to cover turkey. Simmer, covered, over low heat about 30 minutes until tenderloins are done. Remove turkey from pan and chill.

Sauce
1/2 cup plain lowfat yogurt
2 TBS. nonfat sour cream
1/2 tsp. onion powder
1 tsp. curry powder
1/4 cup mango chutney, chopped

Combine remaining ingredients (reserve 2 TBS. chutney). Spoon over tenderloins to completely cover. Chill at least one hour. To serve, spoon remaining chutney over all and slice into medallions. Makes 4 servings.

A ball hit to the left is a hook, a ball hit to the right is a slice, a ball hit straight is a miracle.

Grilled Mustard Chicken

1 cup dry white wine
1/2 cup olive oil
salt, pepper
fresh or dried thyme
1 3-lb. chicken, cut into serving pieces
2 TBS. dry mustard
1 TBS. honey
1 whole clove garlic

Combine wine and oil and garlic in a large bowl. Season to taste with salt, pepper and thyme. Place chicken in mixture at least 1 hour. Remove chicken from marinade, reserving marinade. Broil chicken on both sides in oven or on barbecue grill 35 to 40 minutes. Meanwhile, combine 3 TBS. reserved marinade, dry mustard and honey; cook over low heat for 2 minutes. When chicken is just done, brush with mustard sauce and serve. Serves 4 to 6.

One must not tie life to a single hope, nor golf to a single shot.

Chicken Boursin

1 5-oz. pkg. garlic and herb flavored Boursin cheese
2 chicken breasts, split, skinned and boned
lemon or lime juice
salt, pepper to taste
1 egg, well beaten
flour
dry bread crumbs
1/2 cup butter
1/4 cup oil

Quarter package of cheese and roll each quarter into a finger 1/2 inch thick. Wrap each finger in plastic wrap and chill well. Flatten chicken between 2 sheets of waxed paper and pound until 1/8 inch thick. Sprinkle lightly with juice, salt and pepper. Place cheese fingers lengthwise on long sides of breasts. Roll chicken around cheese to enclose it and secure with toothpicks. Dust chicken rolls with flour, dip in egg and roll in bread crumbs. Chill 1 hour or longer. In a heavy skillet just large enough to hold chicken in 1 layer, sauté the rolls in butter and oil over medium-high heat for 10 minutes per side. Drain on paper towels and serve immediately.
Serves 2-3.

With each golf swing, swing easy but hit hard.

Chicken Hunter's Style

Contributed by
George Bayer
PGA Teaching Professional

George Bayer was the first golf professional at the Incline Village Golf Course, Incline Village, Nevada. He is retired and lives with his wife, Mary Ann in Palm Desert, California.

1/3 cup olive oil
1 large clove garlic, minced
1 4-lb. chicken **or** 4 lbs. chicken parts
1 lb. fresh tomatoes, peeled, chopped **or** 1 1-lb. can tomatoes, undrained
1/2 cup Marsala wine
1 tsp. salt
1/4 tsp. freshly ground black pepper
1/2 tsp. dried oregano
1 large onion, sliced (about 1 cup)
1 large green Bell pepper, chopped
1 stalk celery, chopped
1 carrot, sliced
1/4 lb. fresh mushrooms, sliced **or** 1 4-oz. can mushroom pieces, drained

Cut chicken into serving size pieces and pat dry on absorbent paper. Heat oil in large skillet; add garlic and chicken pieces. Sauté for about 10 minutes, or until evenly browned. Add remaining ingredients, except mushrooms; cover and simmer for 40 minutes, stirring occasionally. (Add a bit of water if the pot gets dry.) Add mushrooms and continue cooking for 15 minutes, until tender. Serve with pasta, polenta, or crusty Italian bread. Serves 4-6.

"Tip from the top. Head movement. The whole golf swing revolves around the head. It is of the greatest importance to keep your head in one place whether it be in driving, ironplay, chipping or putting. Movement of the head is usually caused by anxiety, which means you want to see the results before they happen." George Bayer

Turkey Loaf with Mustard Sauce

Loaf
2 lbs. ground turkey
1 1/4 cups fresh bread crumbs
1/2 cup milk
1/2 cup egg beaters
2 tsp. salt
1/2 tsp. pepper
1 tsp. poultry seasoning
1 tsp. oregano

Mix all ingredients and spread flat about 1 inch thick and about 8 inches wide.

Stuffing
10 oz. chopped drained spinach
1 medium onion
1 clove garlic
olive oil

Sauté onion and garlic in olive oil. Mix with spinach and spread on turkey mixture. Roll to form loaf and bake in loaf pan for 60 minutes at 350°.

Mustard Sauce
1/4 tsp. tarragon
1/2 cup nonfat mayonnaise
1/2 cup nonfat yogurt
2 TBS. Dijon mustard
3 TBS. minced parsley and/or chives
1 TBS. capers

Mix together and serve with turkey loaf. Serves 6-8.

Raspberry Chicken

12 chicken breast halves, skinned, boned
salt, red and black pepper
8 oz. raspberry preserves, unsweetened
4 oz. pineapple juice concentrate
2 cloves garlic, minced
1/2 tsp. curry
1/2 tsp. Tabasco
1 tsp. crushed red pepper
1 TBS. raspberry vinegar
1/2 tsp. sweet basil
1/4-1/2 tsp. chili powder
1 TBS. Dijon mustard

Season chicken breasts with salt and red and black pepper. Mix remaining ingredients in amounts shown or to taste. Place chicken in a baking dish and pour mixture over. Bake in 350° oven for about 30 minutes or until juices run clear.

Duffer's Basic Law: A draw is a shot you don't learn to hit until you start playing a course that doglegs right on every hole.

Patty Sheehan's Scrumptious Salmon

Contributed by
Patty Sheehan
LPGA Professional

In 1984 at the Jack Nicklaus Sports Center in Kings Island, Ohio, Patty Sheehan became the only golfer to win the LPGA Tournament by 10 shots.

salmon filet
mayonnaise
lemon slices
onion
zucchini
summer squash
foil

Lay foil on counter (about 18" long). Put rinsed salmon filet on foil, skin side down. Spread some mayonnaise on salmon. Put 3 slices of lemon on next. Chop bite-sized pieces of onion, zucchini, summer squash and pile those on top of salmon. Fold foil up and around salmon locking all sides so steam doesn't escape. Place on grill and cook for 8 minutes on each side. Open and enjoy.

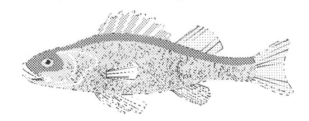

"Golf is like a love affair: If you don't take it seriously, it's no fun; if you do take it seriously, it breaks your heart." Arnold Daly

Roasted Pepper Scallops

1 1/2 lbs. sea scallops
2 TBS. olive oil
zest of one lemon
freshly ground pepper
4 large, red Bell peppers

In a bowl, combine scallops, olive oil, lemon zest and ground pepper to taste. Preheat broiler (or start fire in grill). Cut peppers in half lengthwise and remove stems, seeds and ribs. Place cut side down on a baking sheet. Broil (or grill) until blackened, 6-10 minutes. Transfer to a brown paper bag, close tightly and let cool for 10 minutes. Remove skins and cut peppers lengthwise into 3/4-inch wide strips. Wrap a pepper strip around a scallop to cover completely, overlapping the pepper ends. Secure strip in place by running a skewer through the scallop and pepper. Repeat with the remaining pepper strips and scallops, dividing the wrapped scallops evenly among the skewers. Grill skewers over a medium-hot fire, turning once, until scallops are almost firm to the touch, 1-2 minutes on each side (or 3 minutes per side under broiler). Serve immediately.
Serves 6.

"If you need the ball to stop real fast, when coming out of a sand trap, the backswing should be more upright which will throw the ball high in its flight, resulting in less role when hitting the green." George Bayer

Tuna with Papaya Cilantro Salsa

1 papaya, peeled, seeded, diced
1 medium tomato, peeled, seeded, diced
1 fresh cilantro bunch, chopped
1/2 red Bell pepper, diced
1/2 green Bell pepper, diced
1/2 yellow Bell pepper, diced
2 1/2 TBS. fresh lime juice
1 1/2 TBS. olive oil
4 6-oz. tuna steaks, 1/2-inch thick
9 green onions, cut in 1-inch pieces (diagonally)
Tabasco

Combine first 7 ingredients in a large bowl. Add olive oil and toss to coat. Season to taste with Tabasco. Cover and refrigerate. Can be made 3 hours in advance. Prepare barbecue (medium-high) or broiler. Place tuna on baking sheet and brush with oil. Season with salt and pepper. Grill until just cooked through, 3 minutes per side. Transfer to plates. Grill onions until wilted and golden, about 1 minute. Arrange onions atop each tuna steak. Spoon salsa over and top with cilantro sprigs.

 Suggested Wine: Full-bodied Chardonnay.

Baked Crab

1 med. green pepper, chopped
1 med. onion, chopped
1 cup celery, chopped
1 lb. crab meat (or half crab and half shrimp)
1/2 tsp. Worcestershire sauce
1 cup mayonnaise
1 cup fresh bread crumbs
4 TBS. melted butter

Combine first six ingredients in a casserole. Mix bread crumbs and butter and sprinkle over top of casserole. Bake at 350° for 30 minutes or until browned. Serves 4.

Cynthia's Creole Buttered Shrimp

This dish transports you to South Louisiana. For an easy meal add a salad and hot crusty French bread.

1 lb. uncooked shrimp, shelled and deveined
1/2 cup butter
salt, pepper
2-3 cups hot cooked grits or polenta

Heat butter in a heavy skillet and sprinkle with salt and pepper. Add the shrimp and cook two minutes over low heat. Cover and cook eight minutes, stirring two or three times. Correct seasoning if necessary. Serve a spoonful of hot grits onto the plate, make a well in the center and fill it with hot, buttery shrimp. Serves 4-6.

Margarita Shrimp

3/4 lb. raw shrimp (20)
1 small ripe avocado
1 TBS. finely chopped shallots
3/4 cup heavy cream
2 TBS. finely chopped cilantro
1/4 cup lime juice
salt, pepper
1 TBS. butter
1 TBS. olive oil
1/4 cup tequila
1/8 tsp. red pepper flakes

Shell, devein and butterfly shrimp. Put shrimp in a bowl with lime juice, salt and pepper. Let stand briefly until ready to cook. Peel avocado and cut into 1/2-inch slices. Heat butter and olive oil in a skillet and when it is quite hot but not smoking add shrimp and pepper flakes; stir rapidly, cook 2 minutes. Sprinkle with shallots and cook 10 seconds. Add tequila and cream and cook over high heat about 1 minute. Add salt and pepper to taste. Add avocado and cook just until slices are hot. Using a slotted spoon, transfer the shrimp and avocado pieces to serving dishes. Bring sauce to full boil for 30 seconds, add cilantro. Spoon sauce over the shrimp and avocado. Serve with rice. Makes 4 servings.

 Suggested Wine: A rich and fruity Chardonnay.

Filet of Sole

3 or 4 lbs. of filet of sole	1/2 tsp. ground sage
5 TBS. butter	2 tsp. salt and pepper
2 TBS. minced parsley	1/2 cup dry white wine
1 shallot or green onion, minced	

Put butter in a bowl and stir until soft and foamy. Beat in parsley and onion and sage until light and fluffy. Spread half in bottom of baking dish. Put fish on top in a single layer. Dot with remaining butter. Cover and bake in pre-heated 350º oven for 10 minutes. Remove cover and salt and pepper to taste; add wine. Cover again and bake for another 10 minutes or until fish flakes. Test with toothpick. Serves 6-8.

When coming out of a greenside bunker with a large area of sand to carry, instead of using a sand wedge, use a nine iron. Open the club-face, open your stance and swing through the shot. You'll carry the trap and stop on the green. A pitching wedge works too if the distance you must carry is shorter. Told to an IVGC member by Gary Player.

Divine Fish Divan

1 lb. Orange Roughy (or other white fish)
2 TBS. butter or margarine, melted
1 TBS. lemon juice
1/2 lb. fresh broccoli or asparagus spears, cooked crisp-tender
1/4 cup sour cream
3 TBS. grated Parmesan or 2 TBS. Romano
paprika

Rinse filets, pat dry. Cut into 4 serving size portions. Place fish in single layer in 8 x 12-inch baking dish. Drizzle with lemon juice and butter. Cover and bake in preheated 450° oven 7-8 minutes. Remove fish from oven. Place two spears cooked broccoli or asparagus on top of each filet. Combine sour cream with cheese. Place dollop of cream mixture on top of vegetables in center of filet. Return to oven and bake uncovered 3-4 minutes or until heated through then sprinkle with paprika. Serves 4.

 Suggested Wines: Fumé Blanc or lean crisp style Chardonnay.

Shrimp Creole

1/2 cup onion, chopped
1 clove garlic, crushed
1/2 cup celery, diced
1/4 cup green pepper, diced
2 TBS. olive oil
2 1/2 cups canned tomatoes
1 bay leaf
2 tsp. sugar
2 tsp. parsley, chopped
4 cloves
1 tsp. flour
2 cups shrimp (cooked)
cooked rice

Sauté onions, garlic, celery, and green pepper in olive oil until soft but not brown. Add remaining ingredients except flour and cook over low heat until thick. Remove cloves and add flour dissolved in a little water. Add shrimp and serve over rice. Makes 3 cups or 4 servings.

 Suggested Wine: Pinot Noir.

Salmon In Parchment

For a tasty and very tender fish dish, this is the one you're looking for.

1 6-8-oz. Salmon steak per person (Halibut or Orange Roughy filets if you prefer)
lemon slices
fresh basil, tarragon or dillweed (dry herbs may be used)
season salt
black pepper
enochi (straw) mushrooms
zucchini, julienned
carrots, julienned
butter or vegetable spray
white wine or nonfat milk
parchment paper (aluminum foil may be substituted for quick less-elegant presentation)

Heat oven to 450º. Tear parchment paper (or aluminum foil) off roll in about 8-12-inch pieces. Rub paper with butter and arrange fish steak or filet at upper half. Season with salt and pepper. Place a sprig of fresh herb (or sprinkle dry herb) over fish. Cover with lemon slice. Drizzle lightly with wine or milk. Top with optional few pieces of straw mushrooms, julienned zucchini and/or julienned carrots. Fold paper over fish. Begin folding at open side and continue folding wedges around outside until the package is closed, resembling a half moon shape. Place wrapped fish on cookie sheet and bake in upper half of oven for 20 minutes. Remove from oven and allow to rest 15 minutes. Serve on individual plates in wrapper.

 Suggested Wines: Fumé Blanc or lean crisp style Chardonnay.

Hugh's Barbecue Salmon

cheese cloth
aluminum screen wire and stapler **or** commercial fish rack
6-8 lb. tail end piece salmon

Court Bouillon
2 cups chicken broth
1 cup dry white wine
1/8 cup wine vinegar
1 cup coarsely cut carrots
1 cup coarsely cut onions
2 stalks cut celery
2 sprigs parsley
2 bay leaves
1/2 tsp. pepper
1/2 tsp. tarragon
1/2 tsp. thyme
freshly ground pepper and salt

Remove tail and fins from fish. Split and clean inside. Cut sufficient aluminum screen wire to wrap around salmon plus 2 inches overlapping. Bring broth, wine, vinegar, vegetables and seasonings to boil; simmer 10 minutes; remove from heat and cool. Gather vegetables up in cheese cloth and place into cavity of fish. Place on screen wire and fold over. Staple snugly around all edges. Place on barbecue 12-14 inches above heat and barbecue 20 minutes on each side, basting with court boullion liquid. Closed barbecue recommended. Remove to cutting board, cut screen wire with kitchen shears. Skin will adhere to wire. Remove cheese cloth, carefully lift to a large, warm platter and garnish with lemon and parsley.

Steak Diane

This recipe is especially good with game such as venison or elk.

4 1/2-lb. tenderloin steaks, cut 1/2-inch thick
1 1/2 TBS. green peppercorns
drops of soy sauce
olive oil
butter
1/4 cup shallots or scallions
1/4 cup fresh parsley

1 TBS. cornstarch
1 TBS. Dijon mustard
1 cup beef broth
Worcestershire sauce
1/2 lemon
Cognac, Port, or Madera

Pound steaks to about 1/4-inch thick. Drizzle a few drops of olive oil and soy sauce onto each steak. Crush peppercorns and rub onto the oiled meat. Roll each piece of meat cigar fashion and place covered in the refrigerator for 2-4 hours. Place 1 TBS. butter and some olive oil in a skillet and sauté each steak for a few minutes on each side. Don't overcook. Place steaks on a warming tray in the oven. Sauté shallots in pan. Mix 1 TBS. cornstarch with 1 TBS. Dijon mustard and stir into beef broth. Pour mixture into saucepan with parsley and stir until thickened. Squeeze juice of 1/2 lemon and a few drops of Worcestershire and Cognac into sauce. Pour sauce over steaks, garnish with lots of parsley and serve immediately. Serves 4.

"The person I fear most in the last two rounds is myself." Tom Watson

Butterflied Leg of Lamb

This recipe is easy to do on the grill or in the oven.

1 leg of lamb (allow 1/2 lb. bone-in weight per person)

Marinade
3/4 cup vegetable oil
1/4 cup red wine vinegar
1/2 cup onion, chopped
2 cloves garlic, bruised
2 tsp. Dijon mustard
2 tsp. salt
1/2 tsp. crumbled dried oregano
1/2 tsp. crumbled dried basil
1 bay leaf, crushed
1/8 tsp. freshly ground pepper

Have your butcher bone the leg of lamb and cut into butterfly shape. Keep bones and scraps for soup stock. Combine marinade ingredients in a plastic bag, add lamb, and place bag in a large bowl. Turning occasionally, marinate under refrigeration for 24 to 48 hours, the longer the better. Remove lamb from marinade and broil or barbecue, fat side up 4 inches from heat, for 10 minutes. Turn, baste with marinade, and broil for 10 minutes more. If using the oven, continue roasting in a 425° oven for 10 to 15 minutes or until done to taste. If barbecuing, raise the grill slightly and continue basting and cooking until done to taste. Lamb should be crusty on outside and pink inside.

 Suggested Wines: Cabernet, Merlot or old vine Zinfandel.

Individual Lamb Roasts

This recipe is also good using 1 1/2-inch thick lamb chops.

4 lamb shanks, well trimmed of fat
1 clove garlic, quartered
1/4 cup flour
1 tsp. paprika
1/2 cup lemon juice
2 TBS. grated lemon rind
4 peppercorns
2 tsp. salt
1 TBS. peanut oil
2 bay leaves
white wine (if the lamb gets dry during baking)

Trim the fat from the lamb. Insert piece of garlic into each lamb shank. On waxed paper combine flour, salt, and paprika. Roll shanks in flour mixture until well coated. In skillet, brown shanks well in hot oil and place in 3-quart casserole. Add lemon juice to skillet, stir to loosen brown bits, pour over shanks. Add rind, bay leaves, peppercorns. Bake covered at 350° for 1 1/2 to 2 hours. If it gets dry, add white wine. Serves 4.

 Suggested Wines: Pinot Noir, French Red Rhone or California Rhone style wines, such as Sirah.

Barbecue Leg of Lamb

Leg of lamb, boned and tied
6-7 cloves garlic
salt, pepper
flour

Wipe leg of lamb with damp cloth; sprinkle with salt and pepper and a little flour. Rub well; slash and insert cut pieces of garlic into lamb. Place on spit and baste with the sauce frequently until done, 1 hour and 15-20 min. for medium rare or until meat thermometer reads 145º-150º, well done up to 2 1/2 hours. Use indirect heat with a foil basin under the meat. Maintain a high even heat.

Sauce
3 TBS. Worcestershire sauce
3 TBS. steak sauce
1/4 cup tomato catsup
3 TBS. vegetable shortening
1 TBS. sugar
1 TBS. balsamic vinegar
2 tsp. liquid smoke
1 med. onion, grated
1 tsp. salt
few drops of Tabasco

Heat to boiling.

Golf: The only word in the English language that is always spelled backwards.

Veal Scallopini

8 pieces of lean veal
5 generous pats of butter
1 or 2 TBS. olive oil
1 clove garlic, minced
flour
1/2 lb. fresh mushrooms
1 lemon
4 oz. white wine
4 TBS. chopped parsley
salt and white pepper

Pound veal until very thin. Season with salt and white pepper. Brush through flour, drop into very hot oil in skillet, and brown on both sides. Remove veal from pan and place in warming oven. Cut mushrooms, as you would a pie into small sections, add to skillet and let simmer (covered) for 10 minutes. Draw out oil, then add butter, wine and garlic. Cover and simmer for 15 minutes. Before serving squeeze lemon juice over meat; pour mushroom and onion sauce over meat and sprinkle with parsley.
Serves 4.

 Suggested Wine: Chardonnay, Sauvignon Blanc or light Pinot Noir.

Prime Ribs with Pink & Green Peppercorn Crust

4-rib standing rib roast (about 7 1/2-8 lbs.)

Let rib roast stand at room temperature for 1 hour. Preheat oven to 500°.

Crust
2 tsp. whole allspice berries, crushed
3 TBS. pink peppercorns, crushed lightly
3 TBS. green peppercorns, crushed lightly
3 TBS. unsalted butter, softened
2 TBS. all purpose flour
1 TBS. firmly packed brown sugar
1 TBS. Dijon mustard
1 1/2 tsp. salt

Sauce
2/3 cup dry red wine
2 cups low salt beef broth
1 1/2 TBS. cornstarch
1 TBS. Worcestershire sauce
1 TBS. water

Crust
In small bowl combine crust ingredients, stirring to form paste. Pat beef dry; sprinkle with salt and pepper. Place roast rib side down in a pan and place in hot oven for 30 minutes. Transfer beef to platter; discard drippings. Reduce oven temperature to 350°. Return beef to pan, ribs side down; spread with peppercorn paste. Roast beef 1-1 1/4 hours more, or until a meat thermometer reads 135° for medium-rare. Transfer beef to a cutting board and discard strings. Let beef stand covered loosely, 20 minutes before carving.

Sauce
Skim fat from drippings in roasting pan. Add wine to pan and deglaze over moderately high heat, scraping up brown bits. Boil mixture until reduced by about half and transfer to a saucepan. Add broth and boil 5 minutes. In a bowl dissolve cornstarch in Worcestershire sauce and water and add to pan in a stream, whisking. Bring sauce to a boil, whisking, and boil 1 minute. Season sauce with salt and pepper. Garnish rib roast with rosemary sprigs and serve with sauce. Serves 8.

Filet of Beef

16 filet mignon steaks (1-inch thick, 6-8 oz.)
2 large cloves garlic, crushed
1 TBS. seasoned salt
1/2 tsp. pepper
1/4 lb. butter plus 2 TBS.
4 TBS. brandy
6 TBS. all purpose flour
4 tsp. tomato paste

1 tsp. crushed garlic
1 1/2 cups dry red wine
2 cups chicken broth
1 cup beef broth
1/2 tsp. Worcestershire sauce
4 TBS. currant jelly
1 lb. mushrooms, sliced

Place steaks on work surface in a single layer. In a small bowl, make a paste of 2 cloves garlic, seasoned salt, and pepper. Rub mixture on both sides of steaks. Heat 2 TBS. butter in a large heavy skillet until hot. Sauté steaks over moderately high heat until brown on each side but still raw in middle. Do not crowd or meat will steam. Add butter as needed. Divide steaks between two 9x13-inch casseroles; leave at least 1 inch space between each. Add brandy to skillet. Cook over moderate heat, stirring constantly, scraping up all brown bits. Add 1/4 lb. butter. When melted and foamy stir in flour, reduce heat to low; cook stirring constantly until golden. Stir in tomato paste and 1 tsp. garlic; mixture will be thick. Remove pan from heat and whisk in wine, chicken broth and beef broth. Return to moderate heat and bring to boil, stirring constantly. Reduce heat and simmer 10 minutes. Stir in Worcestershire sauce and currant jelly. When jelly has melted stir in mushrooms. Adjust seasoning. Sauce should be coating consistency. If too thick, thin with broth or wine. Cool completely. Pour over steaks in casserole. Sauce should not come more than 1/2 way up on steaks. May be refrigerated and covered with foil overnight. Before serving bring to room temperature for about 2 hours. Preheat oven to 400°. Bake uncovered for 15-20 minutes for medium rare, 20-25 minutes for medium to medium well. Spoon sauce over steaks to serve. Serves 16-20.

Suggested Wine: A young Cabernet Sauvignon.

Company Casserole

4 cups noodles (1/2 lb.)
1 TBS. butter or margarine
1 lb. ground chuck
2 8-oz. cans tomato sauce
1/2 lb. Cottage cheese (1 cup)

1 8-oz. pkg. soft cream cheese
1/4 cup sour cream
1/3 cup minced scallions
1 TBS. minced green pepper
2 TBS. melted butter or margarine

Early in day, cook noodles as directed and drain. Meanwhile, put butter and chuck in a skillet and sauté until brown. Stir in tomato sauce. Remove from heat. Combine Cottage cheese and the next 4 ingredients. In a 2-quart casserole spread some noodles; dot with cheese mixture, cover with a portion of tomato-meat sauce, repeating layers. Pour melted butter on top. Chill. One hour before serving heat oven to 375º and bake for 45 minutes.

Beef Tenderloin

The theme here is "keep it simple"!

Wash and dry tenderloin. Put in pan and bake 17 minutes at 370º. Cool. Heat oven to 350º and bake 25 minutes, NO MORE. No matter what size, it will be perfectly cooked to medium.

Sherry Glazed Roast Leg of Lamb

1 5-6 lb. leg of lamb
2 cloves garlic, slivered
4-5 fresh mint sprigs, finely chopped
1/2 tsp. salt
1/2 tsp. white pepper
1/2 tsp. ground thyme
1 med. onion, cut into eighths
1/3 cup dry Sherry, can use more
1/3 cup mint or currant jelly

Make several slits on outside of lamb and insert garlic slivers. Combine mint, salt, white pepper, and thyme; rub on roast. Layer onion in a roasting pan; place roast on onions. Put the meat thermometer into meat. Be sure it does not touch the fat or the bone. Bake at 325° for 2 to 2 1/2 hours. Combine Sherry and mint or currant jelly. Glaze roast with Sherry mixture; bake an additional 30 minutes or until thermometer reads 160°. Let stand 10 minutes before carving.

 Suggested Wines: Merlot, Pinot Noir or Zinfandel.

Spicy Beef Tenderloin

1 cup Port wine
1 cup soy sauce (lite)
1/2 cup olive oil
1 tsp. pepper
1 tsp. dried whole thyme
1/2 tsp. hot sauce
4 cloves garlic, crushed
1 bay leaf
1 5-6 lb. beef tenderloin, trimmed

Combine first 8 ingredients; mix well. Place tenderloin in a large shallow pan. Pour wine mixture over top and cover tightly. Refrigerate 8 hours, turning occasionally. Uncover tenderloin; drain off and reserve marinade. Place tenderloin on a rack in a pan; insert meat thermometer, making sure it does not touch fat. Roast at 425° for 45 to 60 minutes or until thermometer registers 140° (rare) basting occasionally with marinade. If you'd like it more well done, roast until thermometer registers 150° for medium rare, or 160° for medium. Remember the meat continues to cook some after it has been removed from the oven. Serves 10-12.

 Suggested Wines: Zinfandel or red Meritage.

Four Peppercorn Pork Roast

4 1/2 lb. boneless pork loin, tied
3 TBS. unsalted butter, softened
2 TBS. all purpose flour
1/4 cup mixed black, white, pink and green peppercorns, crushed coarse

Sauce
1/4 cup all purpose flour
1 3/4 cups chicken broth
2 TBS. red wine vinegar or to taste

Rinse off pork and dry, then season with salt. In a bowl, combine the butter and the flour to make a paste. Coat the top of the pork loin with the paste, and sprinkle the paste with the peppercorns, pressing them in lightly. In a roasting pan, roast the pork on a rack in middle of a preheated 475° oven for 30 minutes. Reduce the heat to 325° and roast the pork for 1 1/2 to 1 2/3 hours more or until a meat thermometer registers 155° to 170°. Transfer the pork roast to a cutting board and let it stand for 10 minutes. Make the sauce while the roast is standing. Pour off all but 1/4 cup of the fat from roasting pan, whisk in the flour and cook the roux over moderate heat, stirring for 3 minutes. Add the broth and 1 cup of water in a stream, whisking, and bring the liquid to a boil. Stir in the vinegar and salt to taste and simmer the sauce until it is thickened to the desired consistency. Remove the strings from the roast and cut the roast into 1/2-inch slices. Arrange the slices on a platter and garnish the platter with fresh rosemary sprigs. Pour the sauce into a sauceboat and serve it with the pork. Serves 10.

 Suggested Wines: Pinot Noir or a spicy style Zinfandel.

Arnold Palmer's Hawaiian Meat Balls

Contributed by
Arnold Palmer
PGA Professional

This recipe is a "favorite" of both Mr. and Mrs. Palmer. If the adage "You are what you eat" holds true, we should all go out and shoot below par golf after trying this recipe.

Meat Balls

1 1/2 lbs. ground beef
2/3 cup cracker crumbs
1/2 cup chopped onion
2/3 cup evaporated milk

1 tsp. seasoned salt
1/3 cup flour
3 TBS. shortening
Sweet-Sour Sauce (see below)

Combine first 5 ingredients; mix lightly but thoroughly. Shape meat mixture into 30 balls. Roll in flour. Brown meat balls in shortening. Drain excess fat. Meanwhile, prepare Sweet-Sour Sauce. Pour over meat balls. Simmer, covered, for 15 minutes. Serves 6.

Sweet-Sour Sauce

1 13 1/2-oz. can pineapple chunks
2 TBS. cornstarch
1/2 cup vinegar
1/2 cup brown sugar

2 TBS. soy sauce
2 TBS. lemon juice
1 cup coarsely chopped green pepper
1 TBS. chopped pimiento

Drain pineapple chunks; reserve pineapple. Measure syrup. Add water to make 1 cup liquid. Blend together pineapple liquid and cornstarch until smooth. Stir in next 4 ingredients. Cook until thickened and clear. Add pineapple, green pepper, and pimiento; mix well. Cover. Simmer over low heat 15 minutes.

"What other people may find in poetry, I find in the flight of a good drive." Arnold Palmer

Julie Inkster's
Chippin' & Pitchin' Meatloaf

Contributed by
Julie Inkster
LPGA Professional

Julie Inkster and her husband, Brian, live in Los Altos, California, where Brian is Head Golf Pro at Los Altos Country Club.

1 1/2 lbs. ground beef
1/4 lb. sausage
1 large egg
1/2 cup cracker crumbs
1 large onion, white, chopped
garlic salt to taste
1/2 tsp. salt
1/4 tsp. pepper
1/2 tsp. celery seed

Put all ingredients in a large bowl and mix in well with hands. Shape in meatloaf style. Bake 45 minutes-1 hour at 350º.

"Quiet your hands during chip and pitch shots. Hit through the pitch shot without letting your wrists break down. You must follow through, equal to the length of your backswing. Now, lets go practice!"
Julie Inkster

Alice's Old English Leg of Lamb

This recipe has been passed down three generations in this family.

4-5 lb. leg of lamb, boneless if desired
1/3 cup butter or margarine, melted
1/2 tsp. garlic powder or 1 clove, crushed
1/2 tsp. thyme leaves, crushed
1/2 tsp. oregano leaves, crushed
1/2 tsp. finely chopped parsley
1 tsp. lemon juice
3/4 cup and 3 TBS. flour
2 cups chicken broth
1 TBS. cornstarch

Add spices and lemon juice to melted butter or margarine. Add flour until very thick, like pie crust. Roll out between 2 layers of waxed paper to a thickness of about 3/16". Refrigerate dough until well chilled. Preheat oven to 425°. Remove all fat from leg of lamb and place dough over, carefully forming around top of leg. Insert meat thermometer. Place on rack in roasting pan. Cook about 20 minutes at 425°. Reduce to 375° and roast until about 180° on the meat thermometer. One half hour before done pour 3/4 cup cold water over meat. Remove from oven when done and cool 10 minutes before slicing. While cooling add 2 cups chicken broth to drippings, scraping pan. Add 1 TBS. cornstarch mixed with 2 TBS. cold water to thicken. Be sure to serve piece of crust with slices.

The Law of Wagering: A sandbagger and your money will soon join forces.

Suebelle's Holiday Ham Glaze

Score ham 1/2 hour before glazing.

Glaze
1 tsp. cardamom, toasted
1 tsp. mustard seed, toasted
1 tsp. fennel seeds, toasted
1/4 tsp. cinnamon
1/4 tsp. ginger
4 tsp. Dijon mustard
1/8 tsp. powdered mustard
brown sugar, to taste
molasses, to taste
1 jar orange marmalade
pineapple slices and juice
1/4 cup bourbon

Toast cardamom, mustard and fennel seeds in a dry, heavy skillet over medium heat about 4 minutes. Grind with a mortar and pestle. Add cinnamon and ginger. Add Dijon mustard and powdered mustard, brown sugar and molasses to taste. Add one jar orange marmalade, pineapple juice and bourbon. Heat in microwave and pour 1/3 of mixture over ham covered with pineapple slices. Bake; baste half way through. After removing ham from oven pour remaining mixture over ham and let stand.

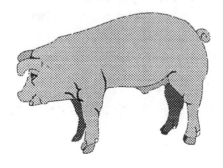

Pasta Primavera

1 lb. fresh asparagus
2 cups fresh broccoli flowerets
1 medium onion, chopped
3 large cloves garlic, chopped
2 TBS. olive oil
1 large carrot, scraped, julienned
1 medium-size sweet red pepper, coarsely chopped
1 medium-size sweet yellow pepper, coarsely chopped
1 cup whipping cream
1/2 cup chicken broth
4 green onions, chopped
2 TBS. chopped fresh basil or 2 tsp. dried whole basil
1/2 tsp. salt
8 ounces uncooked linguine, broken
1/2 lb. fresh mushrooms, sliced
1 cup freshly grated Parmesan cheese
1/4 tsp. freshly ground pepper

Snap off tough ends of asparagus. Cut asparagus diagonally into 1 1/2 inch pieces. Place asparagus pieces and broccoli flowerets in a vegetable steamer over boiling water; cover and steam 6 to 8 minutes or until vegetables are crisp-tender. Remove from heat; set aside. Sauté onion and garlic in oil in a large skillet until tender. Add carrot and chopped peppers to onion mixture; sauté until crisp-tender; remove from heat, drain. Sauté sliced mushrooms and add to mixture. Remove from heat. Combine whipping cream, broth, green onions, basil, and salt in a medium skillet. Cook over medium-high heat 5 minutes, stirring occasionally. Cook linguine according to package directions. Drain well; place in a large serving bowl. Add reserved vegetables and whipping cream mixture; toss gently. Sprinkle with Parmesan cheese and pepper; toss gently. Serve immediately. Serves 8.

Capellini with Clam Sauce

3 TBS. butter
5 TBS. olive oil
5 large garlic cloves, minced
2 10-oz. cans baby clams, reserve juice
1/2 cup bottled clam juice
2/3 cup dry white wine
1 1/2 tsp. dried marjoram, crumbled
1/4 tsp. crushed red pepper
2 TBS. fresh lemon juice
3/4 tsp. grated lemon peel
12 oz. capellini (angel hair pasta)
1/4 cup fresh parsley
thin lemon slices

Melt butter and oil, add garlic and sauté 1 minute. Measure reserved clam juice and add enough bottled juice to make 1 1/2 cups. Add juice, wine, marjoram and red pepper. Boil until reduced to 1 1/4 cup, about 7 minutes. Add clams, lemon juice and peel to skillet. Simmer sauce 2 minutes. Cook capellini according to package directions and add pasta and parsley to sauce.

Penne Pasta Arrebiata

7-9 ripened Roma tomatoes, chopped
4 cloves garlic, minced
1/2 cup white wine
1 1/2 TBS. spaghetti sauce seasoning (Spice Islands)
1 1/2 TBS. Italian herb seasoning
1-2 dried red chili pods, to taste
salt, pepper
3 TBS. olive oil
1 TBS. butter
1/4 cup chopped fresh parsley
1 lb. penne pasta

Put olive oil and butter in large sauté pan; add garlic; brown lightly; add broken chili pods then white wine; let evaporate approximately 6-7 minutes on high heat. Meanwhile start boiling pasta noodles. Add chopped tomatoes to pan along with the seasonings; keep cooking on medium to high heat. When pasta is cooked, drain and add to the sauce; let cook 2-3 minutes. Add fresh parsley. Serves 4.

 Suggested Wines: Chianti or Sangiovese.

Spaghetti in Pomodoro Sauce

3 28-oz. cans crushed plum tomatoes
1/2 cup extra virgin olive oil
3-4 cloves garlic, minced
1 med. onion
3/4 cup red wine
salt, pepper
4 or 5 sprigs fresh basil
3 shakes of red pepper flakes
1 TBS. pesto sauce
1 tsp. spaghetti sauce seasoning
1-2 TBS. Italian herb seasoning
1 lb. spaghetti

Put tomatoes in a blender and puree. In a heavy pot, heat the olive oil. Add the onion and sauté until soft. Add the garlic and sauté until soft. Add the tomatoes and stir to blend. Add the wine, salt and pepper, and basil and stir well. Bring to a boil, lower the heat, and simmer for 25 minutes. The sauce is ready to use, or it can be refrigerated for up to 1 week or frozen up to 3 months. If using immediately, pour over cooked pasta.

Note: You can also add chicken and mushrooms to this sauce. Fry skinless/boneless chicken breasts in a little olive oil until cooked. Then cut the chicken into bite-sized pieces.

Rigatoni
with Vodka-Tomato Sauce

2 TBS. olive oil
1 cup finely chopped shallots*
1/4 tsp. dried crushed red pepper
1/2 cup vodka
3/4 cup whipping cream**
3/4 cup tomato sauce***
8 oz. rigatoni pasta
4 oz. thinly sliced prosciutto, chopped
2/3 cup Asiago cheese (about 2 oz.)
2 TBS. chopped fresh parsley
2 TBS. chopped fresh basil or 1 tsp. dried

Heat oil in heavy large skillet over medium heat. Add shallots and red pepper; sauté until shallots are translucent, about 5 minutes. Add vodka and ignite with long match. Simmer until flames subside, shaking pan occasionally, about 2 minutes. Increase heat to high, add cream and boil until mixture thickens, about 3 minutes. Add tomato sauce; boil until sauce thickens and coats back of spoon, about 2 minutes. Cook pasta in pot, drain, reserve 1/4 cup cooking liquid. Add pasta, prosciutto, 1/3 cup cheese, parsley and basil to skillet and toss to coat. Add reserved pasta cooking liquid if mixture is too dry. Season to taste with pepper. Transfer to large bowl. Sprinkle with remaining 1/3 cup cheese and serve.

   *Instead of shallots you can use garlic.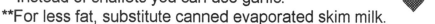
  **For less fat, substitute canned evaporated skim milk.
***Can use chopped tomatoes in a can with liquid.

 Suggested Wines: Sauvignon Blanc or Pinot Blanc.

Pasta with Crab and Artichokes

1/2 cup part-skim Ricotta cheese
1/3 cup lowfat milk
1 tsp. olive oil
2 cloves garlic, minced
1 cup artichoke hearts, canned, drained, cut into bite-sized pieces
6 ounces cooked crabmeat
pinch crushed red pepper
1 tsp. grated lemon peel
salt to taste
1/2 red Bell pepper, roasted, skinned and chopped
2 TBS. parsley, chopped
3 ounces dry pasta, cooked, or 5 ounces fresh
3 TBS. crumbled Feta cheese

In a blender or food processor, blend the Ricotta and milk until very smooth. Set aside. In a nonstick skillet, heat oil and sauté the garlic in it until golden. Stir in the artichokes, crab, crushed pepper and lemon peel. Cook just long enough to heat. Stir in the Ricotta mixture, salt, roasted pepper and parsley. Heat just until the sauce is hot. Toss with the cooked pasta and sprinkle with the Feta. Thin with additional milk if the sauce is too thick. Makes 3 1/2 cups, about 3 servings.

 Suggested Wine: A clean crisp Chardonnay.

Risotto with Scallops

1 cup Arborio rice
2 8-oz. bottles clam juice
1 cup water
1/2 tsp. salt
pepper
1/2 lb. bay scallops (or fresh cleaned calamari)
2-3 cloves shallots, minced, or 2 TBS. minced onion and 1 clove garlic
2 oz. diced Porchini or Portobello mushrooms
3 TBS. olive oil
2 tsp. butter
1/4 cup dry white wine
1/4 cup chopped parsley

In a small sauce pan, heat clam juice, water and salt. Add pepper to taste and retain just below boiling. In a large sauce pan, gently sauté shallots (or onions and garlic) in olive oil plus 1 tsp. butter for 2-3 minutes (until transparent). Add diced mushrooms and continue sautéing for 2 minutes. Dice half of the scallops (or calamari) and add to pan. Sauté for 3 minutes. Add rice and sauté until opaque (about 2 minutes). Add wine and return to slow simmer. Add heated clam juice mixture, 1/4 cup at a time, continuously stirring rice and maintaining a creamy texture. Continue to stir and add liquid until the entire 3 cups (24 oz.) have been added and the rice is cooked. This usually takes 20-25 minutes. The final rice mixture should be creamy. Add more hot water if required. Remove from heat and set aside, covered. In a sauté pan heat 1 tsp. butter and quickly sauté the remaining half of the scallops (or calamari) being careful not to overcook (2-3 minutes). Add sautéed scallops to rice and toss with parsley. Correct seasoning and serve immediately. Serves 2 as a main course or 4 as a side dish.

Tortellini with
Mushrooms and Prosciutto

2 9-oz. pkgs. cheese tortellini
3 TBS. olive oil
1 large onion, chopped
6 oz. thinly sliced prosciutto, chopped
2 TBS. minced garlic
1 tsp. dried crushed red pepper
1 tsp. ground black pepper
1 cup dry white wine
2 cups sliced mushrooms
2 cups chopped red Bell pepper
1 cup chopped green onions
1 cup fresh shelled peas or frozen
1 1/2 cups whipping cream
1/2 cup chopped fresh parsley
1/2 cup chopped fresh basil
1 cup freshly grated Parmesan cheese

Cook tortellini in large pot of boiling salted water until tender but still firm to bite. Drain. Heat oil in heavy large saucepan over high heat. Add onion, prosciutto, garlic, dried red pepper and black pepper. Sauté until onion is golden brown, about 10 minutes. Add wine and bring to boil. Add mushrooms, Bell pepper, green onion and peas and simmer until almost all liquid evaporates, about 5 minutes. Add cream and boil until sauce begins to thicken, about 5 minutes. Add tortellini, parsley, basil and Parmesan. Simmer until sauce coats pasta, about 4 minutes. Season to taste with salt and pepper. Transfer pasta and sauce to large bowl and serve.

Garlic Pasta, No Pesto

1 lb. linguine
10 cloves fresh garlic, coarsely chopped
1/4 cup mild olive oil
1/4 cup extra virgin olive oil
1/2 cup Italian parsley
1/2 tsp. red pepper flakes
2 TBS. capers, drained
salt and pepper to taste

Cook the linguine in plenty of boiling salted water until tender, about
8 minutes. Drain, reserving 3/4 cup of the cooking water. Separately, heat
the olive oil well and sauté the garlic until golden. Add the parsley and
pepper flakes and cook a half minute more. Add the capers and remove
from the heat. Place the pasta in a heated serving bowl and pour the
reserved hot cooking water over it. Toss in the garlic caper mixture and
serve immediately. Serves 4-6.

Pasta Shellina

2 red Bell peppers, sliced thin
8 cloves garlic, diced
1 can ceci beans, drained, rinsed
12 fresh mushrooms, sliced
3 TBS. olive oil
Parmesan cheese
2 TBS. pesto sauce
pasta, linguine, mostaccioli, rigatoni, your choice
10-12 sun-dried tomatoes (in olive oil), chopped

Sauté peppers, garlic, mushrooms, tomatoes and ceci beans in olive oil. Cook and drain pasta noodles. Toss vegetables with pasta and pesto sauce. Sprinkle with Parmesan. Serve immediately.

 Suggested Wines: Light reds such as Chianti, Sangiovese, Pinot Noir or Zinfandel.

Mexican Lasagne

3/4 lb. ground beef
1 tsp. chopped onion
1/2 tsp. garlic salt
1 1 1/4-oz. pkg. taco seasoning
2 8-oz. cans tomato sauce
1 cup Cottage cheese (small curd) **or** nonfat Cottage cheese
1 cup sour cream **or** nonfat sour cream
1 4-oz. can chopped green chilies
1 7-oz. pkg. tortilla chips
8 oz. sharp Cheddar cheese, shredded, **or** lowfat Cheddar

Sauté ground beef, drain excess fat. Add onions, garlic salt, taco seasoning and tomato sauce to the beef. Simmer for 5 minutes. Set aside. In a large bowl, mix Cottage cheese, sour cream and chilies. Set aside. In a deep 2-quart casserole, layer a third of the tortilla chips, half the meat sauce, half the Cheddar cheese, and half the Cottage cheese mixture. Repeat layers. Cover with remaining third of the tortilla chips. Bake at 350° for 35 to 40 minutes. Serves 6.

 Suggested Wine: Zinfandel.

Nevada Noodles

Pasta
1 12-oz. pkg. extra-wide curly egg noodles
4 large eggs (or equivalent low cholesterol egg product)
2 10-oz. pkgs. frozen chopped spinach, thawed and well-drained
4 green onions, sliced
Parmesan cheese
1/8 tsp. ground nutmeg
1/8 tsp. black pepper
1 lb. Mozzarella cheese, shredded
1/4 cup grated Parmesan cheese

Sauce
1 lb. ground turkey
2 tsp. minced garlic
2 28-oz. cans crushed tomatoes
2 tsp. sugar
1 tsp. dried basil
1/2 tsp. dried oregano
1 large bay leaf
1/8 tsp. salt
1/4 tsp. pepper

In a saucepan over medium-high heat, brown turkey, breaking pieces. Drain off excess fat. Stir in remaining sauce ingredients. Bring to boil, reduce heat and simmer uncovered 1 hour until sauce thickens, stirring occasionally. Discard bay leaf. Cook noodles in a large amount of water; drain, rinse and drain again. In large bowl, beat eggs then stir in noodles, spinach, onions and seasonings. Divide one-half of noodles between two well-oiled 9-inch square pans. Top with 1/4 of the sauce, then 1/4 of the Mozzarella. Repeat layers. Sprinkle each casserole with Parmesan. Bake for 30 minutes at 350º. Cool 15 minutes before serving. Serves 8.

Best Spaghetti and Meat Balls

Meat Balls
3/4 lb. ground beef
1/4 lb. lean ground pork
1 cup fine bread crumbs
1/2 cup grated Parmesan cheese
2 TBS. chopped parsley
1 clove garlic, minced
1/2 cup milk
2 beaten eggs
1/2 tsp. salt
dash pepper
1 TBS. salad oil

Sauce
3/4 cup chopped onion
2 cloves garlic, minced
1 tsp. salad oil
2 1-lb. cans tomatoes
2 6-oz. cans tomato paste
1 cup water
1 TBS. sugar
1-1 1/2 tsp. salt
1/2 tsp. pepper
1 bay leaf

Meat Balls
Combine all ingredients except oil, mixing well. Form in small or medium balls. Brown in hot oil or put on oiled cookie sheet and cook at 350° until lightly browned, turning several times. Add to following sauce; cook over low heat 15 minutes. Serve over hot spaghetti. Sprinkle with grated Parmesan. Cook sauce in large pan to hold meat balls. Entrée size, 1 1/2-inch meat balls serve 6. Doubled recipe makes 78 small meat balls and serves 25-30.

Sauce
Sauté onion and garlic in hot oil until just clear and tender, not brown. Add remaining ingredients. Simmer, uncovered, 1 hour. Remove bay leaf.

Spaghetti
Cook 1 8-oz. package spaghetti in boiling water with 1 1/2 tsp. salt to 3 quarts water until tender but firm. Drain. To keep drained spaghetti hot until serving time, place in colander and set over pan containing small amount of boiling water. Coat with 1-3 TBS. salad oil (for 6 servings) to keep strands from sticking. Cover colander.

Seafood Lasagne

White sauce
1/4 cup flour
1/4 cup butter, melted
2 cups milk

To make a white sauce blend flour into butter. Gradually add milk. Cook, stirring constantly, until thickened.

Lasagne
12 lasagne noodles
1 cup chopped onions
2 TBS. butter or margarine
1 8-oz. pkg. cream cheese, softened
1 1/2 cups cream-style Cottage cheese
1 lb. cooked shrimp, shelled, cut in half lengthwise
1 7 1/2-oz. can crabmeat, drained and flaked
1/4 cup grated Parmesan cheese
1/2 cup shredded sharp processed American cheese

2 cups white sauce
2/3 cup dry white wine
1 egg, beaten
2 tsp. crushed basil
1/2 tsp. salt
1/8 tsp. pepper
fresh parsley

Cook noodles according to package directions; drain. Put two layers of three noodles each on bottom of a greased 9x13-inch baking dish. Sauté onion in melted butter until tender. Blend in cream cheese, then add Cottage cheese, egg, basil, salt, and pepper; mix thoroughly. Spread half on top of noodles. Make a white sauce according to the above instructions. Combine white sauce and wine. Stir in shrimp and crabmeat; spread half over Cottage cheese layer. Repeat layers starting with remaining noodles, then Cottage cheese mixture, then seafood mixture. Sprinkle with Parmesan cheese. Bake uncovered at 350º for 45 minutes. Top with American cheese, and bake 2 to 3 minutes until the cheese is melted. Let stand 15 minutes before serving. Garnish with parsley and shrimp. Serves 12.

Roasted Pepper Pasta

2 roasted red Bell peppers **or** 1 chopped red Bell pepper
8-10 cloves roasted garlic
8 Roma tomatoes, chopped
2 TBS. capers
1 8-oz. jar or approx. 20 Kalamata olives, pitted, coarsely chopped
1 cup nonfat sour cream
1 caramelized onion, sliced thinly
meat from large roasted chicken **or** 1 1/2 small chickens, deboned, skinned

Sauté the Bell pepper, garlic and tomatoes. Add capers and olives. Caramelize onions separately in nonfat chicken stock and add to above. Add chicken and sour cream and cook until well blended. Cook your choice of pasta and toss all together.

Guilt-Free Fettuccine

1 14-oz. can chicken broth
1/4 cup all purpose flour
1/4 tsp. garlic powder
1/4 tsp. pepper

1/3 cup plain yogurt
3/4 lb. fettuccine, cooked, drained
6 TBS. Parmesan cheese, grated
3 TBS. fresh parsley, chopped

In a medium saucepan gradually mix broth into flour, garlic powder and pepper until smooth. Over medium heat, cook until mixture boils and thickens, stirring constantly. Remove from heat; stir in yogurt. Pour over pasta and toss along with 4 TBS. cheese. Sprinkle top with parsley and remaining cheese. Serves 6.

Marta Figueras-Dotti's Spanish Paella

Contributed by
Marta Figueras-Dotti
LPGA Professional

This recipe is quite flexible and the meat and seafood can be adjusted as you like.

2 cups rice
6 cloves garlic
1 med. onion
fresh parsley
1/2 chicken
1/2 lb. lamb or pork
1/2 lb. fresh calamari
1 dozen medium shrimp
1/2 dozen jumbo shrimp
2 lbs. clams and mussels (in shell)
1 tsp. saffron
3 bottles of clam juice and water to make 4 cups
1 14-oz. can diced tomatoes **or** 1 lb. ripe tomatoes, peeled and seeded
salt and pepper to taste

Chop onion, garlic and parsley. Peel and chop tomatoes (to peel tomatoes, drop in boiling water for a few seconds then plunge in ice water, and skin comes off easily). In a paella pan, put a little bit of olive oil and mix the garlic, onion, parsley and tomatoes; sauté. Add salt and pepper to taste. Cut all meat and add to the tomato mixture. Add 1/2 cup of water and let cook for 5 minutes. Add rice and stir and let cook for 3 to 5 minutes. In a pot, heat the 3 bottles of clam juice and water until it is boiling. Add to the rice. Add saffron. Add calamari, shrimp, clams and mussels. Cook covered for 20-25 minutes without stirring. Serve, garnished with lemon. Serves 8.

"Stay in the present at all times. If your thought focus is on anything other than the shot you are playing, your performance will suffer. And don't forget to have FUN!" Marta Figueras-Dotti

Fried Rice

For this recipe, the rice is best when cooked at least 4 hours ahead. A day or two ahead is even better. Freshly cooked rice will be too sticky to fry well. Also left over pork roast, chicken or turkey work well or this dish can be made without any meat or shrimp.

4 cups cooked white long-grain rice
4-oz. pork, diced, fat and gristle removed
        and/or 4-oz. chicken breast, diced
        and/or 4-oz. shrimp, diced
1/2 cup egg beaters (or 2 eggs, scrambled)
6 scallions, diced (separate white and green portions)
1/2 cup frozen peas, defrosted under hot tap water (optional)
salt and pepper
1/2 tsp. fresh ginger, minced (optional)
2 TBS. soy sauce
3 TBS. peanut oil (best for high temperature wok cooking)

Add 1 tablespoon oil to very hot wok (large skillet or sauté pan may be used). Fry white portion of scallions and ginger for 2 minutes. Add shrimp and cook about 2 minutes. Add egg beaters and cook until slightly hard. Salt and pepper lightly to taste and remove from wok to large serving bowl. Reheat wok and add two tablespoons oil. Fry diced pork and chicken until cooked through. Salt and pepper lightly. Add rice and fry until rice is heated through. Return egg, shrimp, scallion mixture to wok; add soy sauce (down sides of wok) and peas and mix thoroughly over heat. Remove from heat, toss with green portion of scallions and serve immediately. Serve with a green salad and a hearty bread. Serves 4.

Jazzy Jambalaya

3 TBS. butter
1/2 cup chopped onion
3 garlic cloves, chopped
1/2 lb. smoked sausage (kielbasa), cut into 1/2-inch pieces
1 cup long-grain rice
1 med. potato, peeled, cut into 1/2-inch cubes
2 1/4 cups canned chicken broth
1/2 cup dry white wine
1 4-oz. jar sliced pimientos with juices
1/2 tsp. turmeric
cayenne pepper
1/2 lb. large uncooked shrimp, peeled, deveined
1/2 cup chopped fresh cilantro
fresh cilantro springs

Melt butter in large skillet over medium heat. Add onion and garlic and sauté until just soft, about 5 minutes. Add sausage; sauté until beginning to brown, about 5 minutes. Add rice and stir to coat with pan juices. Mix in potatoes, broth, wine, pimientos with juices and turmeric. Season with salt, pepper and cayenne. Bring to boil; stir well. Reduce heat to medium-low, cover and cook until rice and potatoes are tender and liquid is absorbed, about 20 minutes. Mix in shrimp and chopped cilantro. Cover and cook until shrimp are just cooked through, about 4 minutes. Mound jambalaya on large platter. Garnish with cilantro sprigs and serve. Serves 4.

Pasta Marinara Marsala

1 lb. pasta of choice, fettuccine, linguine, spaghetti
1 lb. fresh ripe tomatoes, peeled and seeded **or** 1 14 1/2-oz. can tomatoes
1 med. onion, diced
1/2 green Bell pepper, diced
2 TBS. tomato paste
1 cup Marsala wine
1 TBS. anchovy paste **or** chopped anchovies (optional)
2 TBS. olive oil
1 tsp. red pepper flakes
Parmesan cheese
salt

Sauté onions and peppers in olive oil until translucent (about 3-5 minutes). Add tomato paste and continue sautéing for 2 minutes. Add wine and simmer one minute. Add tomatoes, anchovy paste, crushed red pepper, and salt to taste. Cover and simmer slowly for 10 minutes. Cook pasta in salted water according to package directions. Toss pasta with sauce and serve immediately with Parmesan cheese.

When putting, look at the color of the grass. The light colored grass is growing away from you. The dark colored grass is growing toward you. If putting into the grain, the ball will roll slowly. When putting with the grain the ball will roll more freely. Adjust your stroke accordingly.

Meatless Portobello Mushroom Stroganoff ♥

6 oz. Portobello mushrooms, sliced
3 TBS. onions, minced
3 cloves garlic, minced
2 TBS. olive oil
1 tsp. butter (optional)
1/4 cup nonfat plain yogurt
1/4 cup dry white wine
1 TBS. cornstarch
2 14 1/2-oz. cans beef broth (Swanson)
2 TBS. water
1 small dill pickle, diced (about 3 inches long)
1/4 cup chopped fresh parsley
9-12-oz. spinach or regular fettuccine
salt and pepper

Put olive oil in pan and sauté onions and garlic over low heat for 2 minutes. Add sliced mushrooms and sauté over medium heat stirring constantly for 2-3 minutes. Add wine and cook additional minute. Add beef broth, pouring through tea strainer to remove any fat. Raise heat to high and reduce sauce until 1/2 of original. Lower heat, dissolve cornstarch in water and stir well into sauce. Add diced pickle and simmer 1 minute and remove from heat. Stir yogurt, butter and parsley into sauce. Salt and pepper to taste. Set aside. Cook fettuccine "al dente" in water which has been salted to taste (it should taste like well-seasoned soup). Drain, but do not rinse. Toss with sauce and serve immediately with crusty bread.

Prawn & Veggie Angel Hair Pasta

Contributed by
Shelly Godeken-Wright
PGA Teaching Professional

1/2 lb. peeled and deveined fresh prawns
2 cloves chopped fresh garlic
1/4 cup chopped green onions
2 TBS. olive oil
1/3 cup white wine
2 cups cut broccoli
2/3 cup sliced fresh mushrooms
2/3 cup sliced fresh tomatoes, seeds removed
1 tsp. chopped fresh basil
1 tsp. chopped fresh oregano
1 tsp. chopped thyme
2 TBS. Parmesan cheese
8 oz. angel hair pasta

Sauté prawns, garlic, green onions and olive oil over medium heat until prawns are pink. Start preparing pasta. Add white wine, broccoli, fresh mushrooms and tomatoes to prawns. Cook while constantly stirring until broccoli is done to desired crispness. Add basil, oregano and thyme (add another 1/4 cup white wine if mixture is dry) and simmer for 2 minutes. Add cooked pasta to mixture and toss adding Parmesan cheese. Serve immediately. Serves 4.

"Free up your swing by allowing your head to come up after impact. Locking your head in place doesn't allow you to use all of your possible clubhead speed, finish completely or get your weight to the left side (for the right handed player). Get the most out of your swing, add distance, be relaxed and balanced." Shelly Godeken-Wright

In The Rough
Veggies & Side Dishes

In The Rough - Veggies & Side Dishes

Cool Carrots

2 lbs. carrots, thinly sliced
1 small green Bell pepper, chopped
1 can tomato soup
1/2 cup salad oil
3/4 cup vinegar
2/3 cup sugar
1 tsp. dry mustard
1 cup finely chopped onion

Cook onions and carrots and green Bell pepper until tender. Drain. Heat oil, sugar and vinegar until sugar dissolves. Add soup and mustard. Pour over carrots and onions and keep in refrigerator. Serve cold. Can be stored several days.

Thy longest drive prevaleth not...if thou fouleth up thy second shot.

Potatoes Gratin Dauphinois

4 cups potatoes, very thinly sliced
1 tsp. salt
1/4 tsp. freshly ground pepper
1/8 tsp. freshly grated nutmeg
1 clove garlic, very finely minced
1 1/4 cups grated Gruyere cheese or Emmenthaler cheese
4 TBS. butter
2 eggs, lightly beaten
1 cup heavy cream
2 TBS. freshly grated Parmesan cheese

Preheat oven to 375º. In a large bowl, toss to coat the potatoes with 1/2 tsp. of salt, 1/8 tsp. of pepper, nutmeg and garlic. Place 1/3 of the seasoned potatoes in the bottom of a well-buttered shallow baking dish, sprinkle with 1/3 of the Gruyere cheese and dot with 1/3 of the butter. Repeat twice. In a small bowl, beat eggs, cream, and remaining salt and pepper. Pour evenly over potato layers and sprinkle with Parmesan cheese. Bake, covered, for 35 minutes. Remove cover and bake for another 10 minutes or until potatoes are softened and top is golden brown and bubbly. Serves 6.

Be decisive. A good player decides on a shot and then hits it.

Zucchini Casserole

2 lbs. zucchini
12 soda crackers, crumbled
2 eggs
1 tsp. Worcestershire sauce
1 cup Cheddar cheese, shredded
salt
pepper
Parmesan cheese
potato chips, crumbled

Wash and slice zucchini into 1/2-inch rounds. Place in a saucepan with
1 inch of salted water. Steam until soft and drain. Mash cooked zucchini and
add eggs, soda crackers, Cheddar cheese, Worcestershire, salt and pepper
to taste. Mix ingredients and place into a glass baking dish. Sprinkle a light
layer of crumbled potato chips and Parmesan cheese on top. Place in oven
and bake at 350° until a knife comes out clean, about 40 minutes. Serves 4.

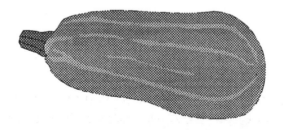

Zucchini Soufflé

3 lbs. zucchini, sliced
7 eggs, separated
3 cups Tillamook cheese, grated
1 large onion, chopped
2 cups bread crumbs
1/4 lb. butter
salt
pepper

Butter casserole and line with 1/2 the required bread crumbs. Par boil zucchini until tender but firm. Place in a strainer to drain. Sauté chopped onion in butter. To the cooked onion add egg yolks, cheese and zucchini. Beat egg whites stiff but not dry and fold into the above mixture. Pour mixture into buttered, crumbed casserole. Top with remaining crumbs. Bake in a moderate oven, about 350° for 30 minutes. Serves 16.

"For the sand shot, start with the stance approximately the width of your shoulders, and in the open position. The ball should be positioned off the left toe. The club face should be in the open position. Hit 3-4 inches behind the ball and follow through. The sand will carry the ball out of the bunker." George Bayer

Joe's Baked Eggplant

1 average-sized eggplant, peeled and cut into 1-inch cubes
1/4 cup onion, chopped
1/4 cup green Bell pepper, chopped
1/4 cup celery, chopped
1 TBS. butter or margarine
1/2 tsp. salt
2 slices white or wheat bread, torn into small pieces
1/2 cup milk
1 egg lightly beaten or equivalent no-cholesterol egg product
1 TBS. chopped pimiento
1/4 tsp. black pepper
1/4 tsp. sage
3/4 cup reduced fat Cheddar cheese, shredded

Sauté or microwave eggplant, onion, green pepper and celery in butter until soft (when microwaving omit butter if desired but add 1-2 TBS. water and cover with waxed paper). Remove from heat. In a bowl, soften bread with milk and egg. Combine vegetable mixture, bread mixture and all remaining ingredients. Blend and then place in a buttered casserole dish. Bake at 350° for 30-45 minutes until center is set. Serves 4.

At high altitude raise oven temperature to 375°.

When contemplating the horrendous lie in which you find yourself, go behind the apparent circumstances of the situation...blame it on the greens keeper.

Rockee's Butter Bean Bake

4-5 cans butter beans
9 TBS. brown sugar
1 can tomato soup (undiluted)
bacon strips to cover

Drain beans and place in 2-quart casserole. Mix brown sugar and tomato soup together and pour over beans. Top with raw bacon slices. Bake at 350° in oven for 1 hour. Serves 6-8.

Cheese Garlic Grits

1 cup grits
1 stick butter or margarine, melted
8 oz. Cheddar or Jack cheese, shredded
1 4-oz. can diced green chilies
2 eggs or equivalent no-cholesterol egg product and milk to make 1 cup
1 clove garlic, minced
paprika or cayenne pepper

Cook grits in 4 cups salted water according to package directions. Add butter, cheese, green chilies, egg/milk mixture, garlic and mix. Put into greased casserole dish and sprinkle with paprika or cayenne pepper. Bake until set at 350°, about 30 minutes. At high altitude raise oven temperature to 375°.

Baked Butternut Squash with Apples

2 1/2-2 3/4 lbs. butternut squash, peeled, quartered lengthwise, seeded, cut crosswise into 1/4-inch slices
2 1/4 lbs. Granny Smith apples, peeled, and sliced
3/4 cup dried currants
freshly grated nutmeg
3/4 cup pure maple syrup
1/4 cup (1/2 stick) butter
1 1/2 TBS. fresh lemon juice

Preheat oven to 350º. Cook squash in large pot of boiling salted water until almost tender (3 minutes). Drain well. Combine squash, apples and currants in 13x9x2 glass baking dish. Season generously with nutmeg, salt and pepper. Combine maple syrup, butter and lemon juice in heavy sauce pan. Whisk over low heat until butter melts. Pour syrup over squash mixture and toss to coat evenly. Bake until squash and apples are very tender, stirring occasionally, about 1 hour. Can be made 1 day ahead. Cover with foil and chill. Rewarm covered in 350º oven about 30 minutes. Serves 12.

There is nothing insignificant in golf—nothing.

Stuffed Mushrooms

12 med. to large fresh mushrooms
1/2 cup pecans, chopped
3 TBS. parsley, chopped
2 tsp. butter
1 tsp. ground cloves (or less)
1/4 tsp. thyme
1/4 tsp. salt
1/8 tsp. garlic powder
1/2 cup heavy cream

Take stems out of mushrooms, put caps in buttered shallow baking dish. Chop stems, place in bowl. Mix in pecans, parsley, soft butter, cloves, thyme, salt and garlic. Place mixture into caps. Pour cream over. Bake in 350º oven for 20 minutes. Baste 2-3 times with juices. Serves 6-12.

Spinach Squash Bake

1/4 cup all purpose flour
1/4 tsp. cayenne pepper
2 cups low fat milk
1/2 cup onion, chopped
3 cloves garlic, minced
1/2 cup grated Gruyere cheese
1 10-oz. pkg. frozen chopped spinach, thawed, drained, squeezed dry
5 cups cooked spaghetti squash
2/3 cup prosciutto, chopped

Combine flour and cayenne in a bowl and gradually add milk. Whisk until smooth. Spray large saucepan with vegetable oil and place over medium heat until hot. Add onion and garlic, sauté 1 minute. Add milk mixture and cook 6 minutes or until thickened, stirring constantly. Add cheese and spinach; stir well. Remove from heat and add the squash and prosciutto. Spoon mixture into a casserole coated with cooking spray. Bake at 375º for 20 minutes. Serves 6.

To cook spaghetti squash
Cut squash in half lengthwise. Remove seeds. Place squash into pan, cut sides down and add about 1 inch of water. Bake at 350º until squash is tender when pricked with a fork. Add more water as necessary. When done, cool. Scrape the pulp with a fork to separate from the skin.

Chilies Rellenos

4 Poblano, Pastilla or Anaheim chilies
2/3 cup grated Jack cheese
2/3 cup grated Mozzarella cheese
1/2 cup crumbled Feta cheese
1/2 cup frozen whole kernel corn

Mix together the cheeses and corn. Roast the chilies under broiler until skin is charred. Place chilies in paper bag for about 10 minutes. Remove skin from chilies; cut a slit in each chili and carefully remove seeds. Fill chilies with cheese mixture; place on baking sheet and broil until cheese melts and chilies are warmed through. Serve with salsa. Serves 4.

Herb Topped Tomatoes

These tomatoes go especially well with beef steaks or lamb.

2 large tomatoes
2 TBS. fine dry bread crumbs
2 TBS. Parmesan cheese, grated
1 TBS. butter, margarine or olive oil
1/2 tsp. dried basil, oregano, or thyme
1/8 tsp. pepper
dash garlic salt or onion salt

Remove stems and cores from tomatoes; halve tomatoes crosswise. Place cut side up, in a baking dish. Combine bread crumbs, Parmesan cheese, butter or oil, herbs, pepper and garlic salt or onion salt. Sprinkle atop tomatoes. Bake at 375° for 15-20 minutes or until heated through. Serves 4.

Old Bay Potatoes

This lowfat version of the French fry will satisfy your craving for the real thing.

1 lb. potatoes
Old Bay Seasoning
seasoned salt
cooking spray

Cut potatoes into 1/4-inch slices. Place on cookie sheet; spray potato slices lightly with vegetable oil spray. Sprinkle with Old Bay Seasoning and seasoned salt. Turn slices and repeat with spray, Old Bay, and seasoned salt. Bake in 400° oven for 20 minutes; turn and bake another 20 minutes or until golden brown. Serve immediately.

Zucchini Corn Casserole

1 lb. zucchini, sliced thin
1 onion, chopped
1 1/2 cups creamed corn
2 eggs

1/2 cup Cheddar cheese
2 TBS. oil or butter
cracker crumbs
shredded cheese for topping

Boil zucchini until just tender, drain. Sauté onions in 2 TBS. oil or butter. Add to creamed corn. Beat eggs well. Add 1/2 cup cheese. Mix all together. Put in greased casserole and bake at 300° for 1 1/2 hours. Half hour before done, mix cracker crumbs, butter and a little shredded cheese in a pan. Put on top of casserole and continue baking until cheese melts. Serves 6.

Southern Corn Fritters

Fritters are an old fashioned favorite and are good when drizzled with maple syrup or just eaten plain as a side dish with meats or seafood. A great substitute for French fries.

3 TBS. butter or oil
1/2 cup red Bell peppers, diced

Sauté slowly and let cool.

2 cups fresh or frozen corn
3-4 scallions
3 eggs **or** 3/4 cup egg substitute
1 cup milk
1 1/2 cups flour
1/2 cup yellow cornmeal
1 TBS. double acting baking powder
1 tsp. salt
1/4 tsp. cayenne
1/2 tsp. pepper
3 oz. ham, diced

Sift flour and yellow cornmeal together. Mix ham and dry ingredients together; add 3-4 chopped scallions. Blanch corn 3-4 minutes; cut corn off of the cob and add to mixture. Add 3 eggs or 3/4 cup egg substitute, milk and peppers and stir lightly. Let batter rest for 1 hour; adjust seasoning and texture with flour, then spoon into 350° oil. Fry until golden brown.

Italian Style Mushroom Casserole

This is a great way to use that extra Italian spaghetti sauce.

2 large green Bell peppers, seeded
1 lb. mushrooms, sliced
1 med. onion, diced
1/2 cup oil or butter
1 cup Italian tomato sauce
6 slices soft Provolone cheese

Cut peppers into strips. Sauté onions and peppers in oil until onions are clear. Sauté mushrooms. Place mixture into casserole dish. Pour Italian sauce over mixture and cover with cheese. Broil until cheese browns partially. Serves 4.

The General Law of Strategy: The strategic approach you engineered to bring the course to its knees will collapse on the first hole.

Sweet and Savory Bell Peppers

This is good served with a crusty bread as a first course or light entrée.

1 large onion, sliced thin
2 garlic cloves, chopped
1 TBS. unsalted butter
1 TBS. olive oil
1 red Bell pepper, sliced
1 yellow Bell pepper, sliced
1 orange Bell pepper, sliced
2 tsp. capers, chopped
1 can sliced black olives
2 TBS. pine nuts
1/4 cup golden seedless raisins soaked in 1/4 cup boiling water, 15 minutes

In a large skillet, sauté the onions in butter and olive oil over moderate heat until clear. Add the Bell pepper rings and sauté mixture over high heat for 1 minute. Add garlic and sauté for 1 minute over moderate heat. Add the raisins with soaking liquid, capers and olives. Cook mixture covered for 2 minutes and stir in pine nuts. Continue cooking covered until Bell peppers are cooked. Serves 2.

Remember... it's a golf swing...not a golf hit.

Cauliflower with Rye Crumbs and Cheddar Cheese

2 slices of rye bread, ground fine in a food processor
1 TBS. minced onion
1/2 stick (1/4 cup) unsalted butter
1/4 cup flour
4 cups milk
3 cups grated sharp Cheddar
1 1/2 heads of cauliflower (with or without greens), about 3 1/4 lbs. cut into 2-inch flowerets and the greens sliced thin
white pepper to taste

Toast the bread crumbs at 350° for 3-5 minutes or until golden; let them cool. The bread crumbs may be made 1 week in advance and kept in an airtight container. In a saucepan cook the onion in 3 TBS. of the butter over moderately low heat stirring until it is softened. Stir in the flour and cook the roux over low heat, stirring for 3 minutes. Remove the pan from the heat and add the scalded milk in a stream, whisking vigorously until the mixture is thick and smooth. Simmer the sauce, stirring occasionally, for 10 minutes. Add the Cheddar and cook the sauce, stirring until the Cheddar is melted. Season the sauce with salt and the white pepper and let it cool. Cover the surface with plastic wrap. The sauce may be made 2 days in advance and kept covered and chilled. Reheat the sauce in a saucepan over moderately low heat before continuing with the recipe. In a kettle of boiling salted water cook the flowerets for 5 minutes, add the greens and cook the mixture for 3-4 minutes or until the flowerets are tender. Drain the cauliflower; plunge it into a bowl of ice water to stop the cooking. Drain. Pat cauliflower dry with paper towels and transfer it to a buttered flameproof 2-quart baking dish. In a small bowl toss the bread crumbs with the remaining 1 TBS. butter, melted; pour the cheddar sauce over the cauliflower and sprinkle the cauliflower with the bread crumbs. Brown the bread crumbs under a preheated broiler about 4 inches from the heat. Serves 8.

Nonna's Artichoke Patties

2 large artichokes
2 cloves garlic, chopped
2 eggs
2 TBS. olive oil
salt
2 TBS. parsley
2 TBS. fresh Parmesan cheese, grated

Precook artichokes. Scrape meat from artichoke leaves and chop heart.
Combine with garlic, eggs, salt, parsley and cheese. Stir. With a large
spoon drop into sauté pan with olive oil. Sauté until set and golden brown.
Turn and brown other side. Serves 2-4.

Kiwi Salsa

Kiwi Salsa is a good accompaniment to grilled chicken or fish.

4 ripe Kiwis, peeled, diced
3 TBS. green onions, chopped
1 TBS. orange zest, finely chopped
1/2 cup jicama, peeled, diced
2 jalapeños, seeded, chopped
1/2 cup red Bell pepper

2 TBS. fresh lime juice
2 TBS. orange juice
1 TBS. honey
2 TBS. olive oil
2 TBS. fresh mint, finely chopped
salt, pepper

Mix kiwis, onions, orange zest, jicama, jalapeños and red Bell pepper.
Whisk juices with honey and slowly whisk in oil and salt and pepper. Toss
with Kiwi mixture. Add mint and mix well.

Wild Rice & Mushroom Casserole

1/4 cup butter
1/2 cup wild rice, rinsed and drained
1/4 cup brown rice
1/3 cup chopped onion

1/2 lb. mushrooms, sliced
1/3 cup pine nuts
2 cups chicken broth

In a large ovenproof skillet, melt the butter. Sauté onion over medium heat until soft; add mushrooms and cook until tender; add rice and stir to coat grains; add pine nuts and cook a few minutes more. Pour the broth over the rice mixture and cover tightly. Bake in 325° oven for 1 1/2 hours or until rice is tender. Serves 8.

Marilyn's Cranberry Ice

This is a great accompaniment to Thanksgiving or Christmas turkey. Make this a tradition at your house.

1 12-oz. bag cranberries
2 cups water
2 cups sugar
1 lemon

Cook cranberries in 2 cups of water until they pop, about 10 minutes. Press through colander or food processor. Add 2 cups sugar to pulp; cook over slow heat to melt sugar. Cool. Add juice of one lemon. Put in loaf pan; place in freezer. When barely frozen, stir once. Serve in sherbet glasses. Serves 8.

Cheese Soufflé

10 slices white bread
1 lb. Cheddar cheese, grated
4 eggs
3 cups milk
1 1/2 tsp. salt
1/4 tsp. pepper
1 tsp. dry mustard

Grease 2-quart casserole. Cut crusts off bread. Butter and cut each slice into thirds. Grate cheese. Beat together 4 eggs, milk, salt, pepper and mustard. Layer bread and cheese to top. Pour egg mixture over. Cover and refrigerate 24 hours. Bring to room temperature. Bake at 350º for 60-70 minutes uncovered. Will hold at low temperature for 30 minutes. Serves 6.

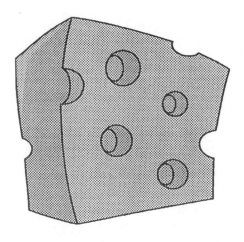

Mexican Hominy

2 15-oz. cans of white or yellow hominy or mix
1 cup yellow onions, chopped
1 cup green Bell pepper, chopped
2 cloves garlic, minced
1 lb. mild Cheddar cheese, sliced
1/2 cup jalapeño peppers, sliced in chips (gringos should use 1/4 cup)
1 cup mild Cheddar cheese, grated

Drain liquid from canned hominy. Sauté onions, peppers and garlic in olive oil until soft and clear. Mix hominy with sautéed ingredients. In a 2-quart casserole dish layer hominy mix with cheese and jalapeño peppers until layers are within 3/4 inch of top of dish. Place in preheated 350° oven for 30 minutes; take out and cover with grated cheese; place back in oven until cheese is melted. Serve as a side dish. Serves 8.

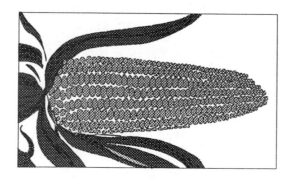

Green Chili Pie

1 large tortilla
1/2 lb. Jack cheese, grated
1/2 lb. Cheddar cheese, grated
4 eggs
8 oz. sour cream
4 oz. Ortega green chilies, chopped
1/2 cup chopped onions
Lawry's seasoned salt
paprika

Butter a 10-inch pie plate and line with tortilla. Beat eggs with sour cream and add green chilies. Grate two kinds of cheese and mix together. To assemble, place 1/2 grated cheese mixture over tortilla; sprinkle with onions and salt. Pour egg mixture over top of cheese. Add remaining cheeses, seasoned salt and paprika. Bake 1 hour at 325º. Let set 10 minutes before cutting.

God grant me the Serenity to accept things I cannot change, Courage to change the things I can, and enough cash for the best golf lessons money can buy.

Roasted Shallot and Sesame Asparagus

♥

2 1/2 lbs. asparagus, trimmed and peeled
1 1/2 TBS. olive oil
2 TBS. minced shallots
2 TBS. sesame seeds, toasted
fresh lemon juice to taste

In a large shallow baking dish toss the asparagus with the oil, coating it well. Bake it in a preheated 500° oven, shaking the dish about every 2 minutes for 6-8 minutes or until almost done. **Do not overcook.** Sprinkle the asparagus with the shallots and the sesame seeds. Bake about 1 minute or until it can be pierced with a fork. Sprinkle with the lemon juice and salt to taste. Serves 8.

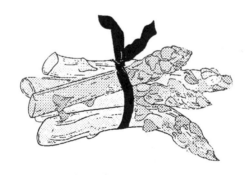

Green Chili Rice

3 cups cooked rice
1 4-oz. can diced green chilies
2 cups sour cream
1 cup shredded Jack cheese

Layer ingredients in a buttered casserole dish. Bake at 350° until hot all the way through. Serves 6-8.

Mary Ann's Baked Lima Beans

1 lb. bag large lima beans
1 cup light brown sugar
2 tsp. French's light mustard
1 bottle Heinz catsup
1 small onion, diced
1/2 lb. sliced bacon, cut up

Boil 1 lb. large lima beans for approximately 3 hours; drain. Save 1 cup liquid to add to beans as they cook; pour into a 2-quart baking casserole and add brown sugar, mustard, catsup, onion, bacon and bake in 350° oven for approximately 2 1/2 hours.

Holiday Sweet Potatoes

1 29-oz. can and 1 16-oz. can sweet potatoes, drained and mashed
1 cup evaporated milk, regular, lowfat or skimmed
1/2 cup sugar
3/4 stick butter or margarine
2 eggs or equivalent no cholesterol egg product

Topping
1 cup crushed corn flakes cereal
1/2 cup coarsely chopped pecans
1/2 cup brown sugar
1/2 stick butter or margarine

Beat butter until smooth and creamy; add milk, sugar, and eggs. Beat again until blended. Add potatoes and blend. Bake in a buttered casserole dish (8x12 rectangular) at 400º until center is set, about 30-40 minutes. Sprinkle on topping and bake another 10 minutes. Serves 10.
At high altitude increase oven temperature to 425º. For a lower fat casserole reduce the amount of butter as desired.

They say that trees are 90% air, but it's still best to stay out of the trees.

Plum Chutney

Contributed by
Dale Shaw
LPGA Professional

2 cups chopped plums (other fruit may be used, peaches, pears, prunes)
2 cups diced apples
1 8-oz. pkg. dried apricots (soaked overnight)
1 14-oz. can pumpkin
1 lb. brown sugar
2 tsp. cayenne pepper
1/4 tsp. garlic powder
1 oz. ginger (crystallized best)
1 cup cider vinegar
1/4 tsp. salt
1/4 lb. light raisins

Boil fruit with a little water until tender and mash. Add all other ingredients except the raisins. Bring to a boil, then simmer gently until a good consistency for chutney. Let it cool a little, then mix in the raisins.

"The golf swing should be rhythmic, fluid and free of effort. This is accomplished by swinging from the body out to the clubhead. By this I mean the body is the engine of the swing. The arms, hands, and club are attached to the shoulders and will move in a swinging action by "following" the body both on the back and the forward swing. The motion must be complete to create this as the clubhead is being "pulled" through the hitting area. Ideally, it is a turn-turn. Start your backswing by turning your back to the target, then face the target with your body (knees, hips, shoulders and head) in a one-two tempo. Two things to remember: the target is your goal and the ball doesn't count in the swing." Dale Shaw

Beans with Rice

1 1/2 cups brown or white rice
1-2 cloves garlic, crushed
1 onion, coarsely chopped
2 TBS. oil
1 med. zucchini, coarsely chopped
2 med. tomatoes, finely chopped
1/2 tsp. oregano
1 16-oz. can any type beans, drained and rinsed
1/2 cup shredded cheese (optional)

Cook rice. Sauté garlic and onion in oil; add zucchini, tomatoes, and oregano. Cover and simmer about 5 minutes. Add beans and simmer until heated. Pour over rice and sprinkle with cheese. Serves 8.

Baked Barley

This recipe is also good topped with steamed zucchini and cheese.

1 onion, diced
1/2 lb. mushrooms, sliced
5 TBS. butter
1 cup barley
1 can water chestnuts, sliced, drained
2 1/2 cups beef broth

Sauté onion and mushrooms in butter. Add barley and brown, add water chestnuts. Place in casserole. Stir in broth. Bake 1 hour at 350º.

Greek Style Green Beans

1 lb. green beans, fresh
1/2-1 cup vegetable stock
1 onion, chopped or sliced
1 clove garlic, minced
1/2 tsp. dried oregano (optional)
3/4 cup tomatoes, peeled, seeded, diced
1 TBS. tomato puree (optional)
salt, pepper

Drop green beans into large pot of salted water and cook until al dente. Drain and refresh in ice water. Set aside. Bring vegetable stock to a boil and sauté onion and simmer until tender. Add garlic, oregano, tomatoes and puree; simmer 5 minutes. Add green beans, simmer 5-7 minutes or until tender. Season with salt and pepper. Serves 4.

Crustless Spinach Quiche

1 TBS. oil
1 onion, chopped
1 10-oz. pkg. frozen spinach
5 eggs
3/4 lb. Monterey Jack cheese

Preheat oven to 350º. Butter 9-inch quiche pan. Heat oil in skillet. Sauté onion until wilted. Add spinach and cook until excess moisture is evaporated. Cool. Beat eggs; add cheese to eggs then add spinach. Season with salt and pepper. Turn into quiche pan. Bake for 40-45 minutes. Can sprinkle Parmesan cheese on top before baking. Serves 8.

Dilled Potatoes Vinaigrette

1 lb. small red boiling potatoes, scrubbed
1/4 tsp. Dijon style mustard
1 TBS. white wine vinegar
1 1/2 tsp. dry Vermouth or dry white wine
2 TBS. olive oil
1/4 cup minced fresh dill

Cut the potatoes lengthwise into fourths; place in a steamer and steam over boiling water, covered for 7-10 minutes, or until they are just tender. In a small bowl whisk together the mustard, vinegar, Vermouth and salt to taste. Add the oil in a stream, whisking until it is emulsified. While the potatoes are still warm add to the dressing and toss gently with dill and pepper to taste until they are coated well. Let the potato mixture stand, tossing it occasionally, for 30 minutes. Serve at room temperature. Serves 4. Potato mixture can be made the day before and covered and chilled overnight. Be sure to let the potato mixture stand at room temperature before serving.

To hit a bad approach is human. To blame it on a bad lie is even more human.

In The Water Hazard
Soups & Stews

In The Water Hazard - Soups and Stews

Soup Au Pistou

4 oz. dried white beans
2 small carrots, peeled, diced
2 small potatoes, peeled, diced
1 lb. tomatoes, peeled, cored, seeded, chopped
1 onion, peeled, chopped
1 leek, white and tender green parts quartered, diced
1/4 lb. green beans, ends snapped, cut crosswise in 1/2-inch lengths
2 small zucchini, diced
1 cup elbow macaroni
4 cloves garlic, peeled
1 packed handful of fresh basil leaves, washed, dried
1 cup grated Reggiano Parmesan cheese
1/2 cup olive oil
bouquet garni: 12 sprigs parsley, pinch of thyme, 1 bay leaf, salt, pepper

Soak beans overnight in water and drain. Put in large pot with 6 cups of water. Bring to a boil and simmer for approximately 1 hour until tender. Drain, discard liquid. Put carrots, potatoes, tomatoes, onions, leeks and bouquet garni in a pot with the cooked beans; add 10 cups of water. Add salt and pepper and bring to a boil; reduce heat and simmer for 30 minutes. Add green beans and zucchini and macaroni and cook for approximately 15 minutes or until macaroni is al dente. Discard bouquet garni. Taste and season. While soup is cooking, prepare pistou. Pound garlic, basil, salt and fresh pepper to a paste in large mortar and pestle or process in a food processor. Work in some of the Parmesan until you have a very stiff paste adding oil and grinding in more Parmesan until the consistency is a fluid paste. Do not add olive oil too quickly or mixture will separate. Ladle hot soup into bowls and place a dollop of pistou in center and sprinkle with Parmesan. Serves 6.

Crab & Artichoke Bisque

1/4 lb. butter
2 tsp. tarragon leaves
1 small onion, diced
1/2 red Bell pepper, diced
1/2 green Bell pepper, diced
3 ribs celery, diced
2 TBS. garlic, chopped
4 oz. flour
1 8-oz. jar artichoke hearts, quartered with liquid
1 quart half & half
1 quart skim milk
2 TBS. Spice of New Orleans or Old Bay Seasoning
1 Knorr's seafood bouillon cube
1 cup crabmeat
4 green onions, chopped
Tabasco & Worcestershire sauce to taste

Sauté first 7 ingredients until vegetables soften. Add flour, cook and stir constantly for 5 minutes. Add brine from artichokes, milk and half & half. Cook and stir over medium heat for about 10 minutes or until sauce coats back of spoon. Add 2 TBS. Spice of New Orleans, bouillon, artichoke quarters, crabmeat, green onion and season to taste with Tabasco and Worcestershire sauce. Serves 6-8.

The most difficult lie in golf is reporting your score to an opponent who has been counting.

Golfer's Gumbo

1/4 lb. bacon, cut in 1-inch pieces
2 lbs. okra, cut in 1/2-inch pieces
2 med. onions,diced
2 stalks celery, diced
5 cloves garlic, minced
1 TBS. parsley
1 1-lb. can whole tomatoes
2 cups boiling water
2 cups beef broth
3 TBS. flour
1 cup cold water
salt, pepper
1 1/2 lbs. shrimp, shelled, deveined and cut in 1-inch pieces
hot cooked rice

Fry bacon until crisp in large kettle. Reserve bacon drippings. Sauté okra in half of reserved drippings, stirring constantly, about 10 minutes. Place okra in kettle with bacon. Add remaining drippings to skillet and sauté onions and celery until onions are tender but not browned. Add garlic and parsley, mix well, then add half of tomatoes. Cook, stirring occasionally, until tomatoes darken in color somewhat. Add remaining half tomatoes and simmer 5 minutes. Pour into kettle with okra. Add 1 cup boiling water and mix well. Add 2 cups beef broth. Stir over medium heat until gumbo comes to boil. Reduce heat and simmer 20 minutes. Add last cup boiling water and cook 10 minutes. Blend flour with cold water until smooth. Add to boiling gumbo and let come to a boil again, stirring constantly. Season to taste with salt and pepper. Add shrimp and simmer 5 minutes. Let stand 20 minutes before serving or refrigerate overnight and reheat. Serve hot gumbo over hot rice in soup plates. Serves 6-8.

Potato Leek Soup

3 leeks, minced
1 med. onion, chopped
4 med. potatoes, sliced fine
4 cups chicken broth

1-2 cups cream
salt, pepper
freshly chopped parsley

Mince the white part of 3 medium leeks and chop onion. Peel and slice very fine four medium potatoes. Place in saucepan with four cups chicken broth. Simmer the vegetables covered until tender. Put into blender and puree. Add 1-2 cups cream. Salt and pepper to taste. Serve with fresh parsley sprinkled on top (may use chives or watercress). Serve very hot or very cold. Serves 4-6.

Asparagus Soup

1/4 cup unsalted butter
1 onion, finely chopped
1 celery stalk, chopped
4 cups chicken stock
salt, white pepper

3 lbs. asparagus, trimmed, 1-inch pieces, tips saved
2 baking potatoes, peeled, 1-inch cubes
2 TBS. fresh basil, finely chopped
2 cups heavy cream (or evaporated skim milk)

In a large saucepan, melt butter over medium heat. Add onion and celery and sauté until translucent, 2-3 minutes. Add stock, asparagus stalks, about 2/3 of tips, potatoes and basil. Bring to a boil, reduce heat, cover and gently simmer until vegetables are tender, about 20 minutes. In small batches, puree soup in a blender, strain and return to pan. Stir in cream, season to taste with salt and pepper and warm over low heat. Meanwhile bring a small saucepan of water to a boil. Add reserved tips and cook until tender, 3-4 minutes. Drain, serve soup immediately and garnish with tips.

Broccoli Cream Soup

2 pkgs. frozen chopped broccoli, thawed
1/4 cup chopped onion
2 cups chicken stock
2 TBS. butter
1 TBS. flour
1 tsp. salt
1/8 tsp. mace
2 cups half & half
pepper

Bring broccoli, onion and chicken stock to a boil. Simmer 10 minutes or until broccoli is tender. Whirl in a blender. Melt butter, add flour, salt, mace, pepper and stir until smooth. Slowly stir in half & half, then add broccoli puree. Cook over medium heat and stir. Season to taste.

Golden Cheese Soup

1/4 cup water
2 TBS. butter
1 10-oz. pkg. frozen corn
1/2 cup shredded carrot
1/2 cup shredded Cheddar cheese
1/2 cup shredded Provolone cheese

1/4 cup chopped onion
1/2 tsp. pepper
1 cup broccoli flowerets
2 cups milk

Bring water, butter, corn, carrots, onion and pepper to boil; cover and simmer 10 minutes. Stir in soup, milk, cheeses and broccoli. Heat, stirring constantly, while cheese melts. Do not boil. Serves 4-6.

Steve's Cioppino

For cioppino, use firm flesh fish such as halibut, red snapper, orange roughy, scallops, uncooked shrimp, lobster, calamari or whatever is fresh and available.

3 lbs. fresh fish, cut into 1-inch cubes
16 little neck clams, well scrubbed
16 mussels, well scrubbed
1 med. onion, diced
3 leeks, cleaned, thinly sliced
      (white and light green parts only)
1/4 cup minced fresh fennel
3 cloves garlic, minced
3 cloves garlic, whole
1 lb. ripe tomatoes, peeled, seeded, diced
      or 1 14 1/2-oz. can tomatoes
1/2 cup dry vermouth (or dry white wine)
1 loaf French bread, sliced & toasted

2 TBS. tomato paste
2 tsp. saffron
1/4 tsp. celery seed
1/4 tsp. crushed red pepper
2 crushed bay leaves
1 tsp. orange zest
salt
olive oil
4 cups bottled clam broth

In a large stock pot, add 3 TBS. olive oil and sauté onions, leeks and fennel until translucent (about 5 minutes). Add tomato paste and continue cooking about 1 minute. Add wine and simmer one minute. Add tomatoes, saffron, minced garlic, celery seed, red pepper, bay leaves, orange zest, and clam broth. Cover and simmer slowly for 10 minutes. This broth can be prepared several hours or days ahead of time and refrigerated until needed. Toast bread slices well and let cool and harden on a rack. Rub each slice with raw garlic. Bring broth to a boil. Add fish, clams and mussels and simmer covered for 10 minutes. Arrange garlic toast in bottom of individual bowls and serve cioppino over toast. Serves 6-8.

Cream of Zucchini Soup

3 cups sliced zucchini
1/2 cup white wine
1 TBS. minced onion
1 tsp. Season All
1/2 tsp. parsley flakes
1 tsp. chicken stock base
2 TBS. butter
2 TBS. flour
1 tsp. chicken stock base
1/4 tsp. Bon Appetit
1 cup milk
1/2 cup light cream or Mocha Mix
pepper
Tabasco

Combine zucchini, wine, onion, Season All, parsley, and chicken stock base and cook until zucchini is tender and only a small amount of liquid is left. Blend in a blender. Combine 2 TBS. butter, 2 TBS. flour, 1 tsp. chicken stock base, pepper and 1/4 tsp. Bon Appetit. Blend well over medium heat. Add 1 cup of milk, 1/2 cup cream or Mocha Mix. Simmer and stir until thick. Add zucchini, mix well. Season to taste with Tabasco and pepper. Add more milk if too thick. Can serve cold or hot. Makes 1 quart.

Keeping together all the components of your good golf swing is like corralling feathers in a wind storm.

Thelma's Chili

4 lbs. hamburger, browned
1 15-oz. bottle Heinz Chili Sauce
2 30-oz. can chili beans
1 30-oz. can kidney beans
2 TBS. Kitchen Bouquet
1 15-oz. can tomato sauce
1 large onion, chopped
2 2 1/2 size can tomatoes, chopped
2 pkgs. Schilling chili seasoning
dash of crushed red pepper

Place all ingredients in a large pot; cook 4-5 hours over low heat; stir often.
Season to taste.

 The law of Scoring: You never get what you want...you get what you get.

Mulligan Minestrone

Stock
1 lb. pink beans
4 quarts water
4 marrow beef bones, 3 inches long
4 slices beef shank, 1 inch thick

Cooked Vegetables
4 TBS. olive oil
2 large onions, diced
2 cups diced carrots
2 cups diced celery
2 cups diced leeks
1 1-lb. can solid pack tomatoes
2 tsp. salt

Raw Vegetables
3 large potatoes, diced
2 cups green beans, 2-inch pieces
4 small zucchini, sliced
3 cups shredded white cabbage
1/2 cup macaroni
1/2 cup chopped parsley
1 clove garlic, minced
2 TBS. dried basil
2 TBS. olive oil
grated Parmesan cheese

Prepare stock: Cover pink beans with water; bring to boil for 2 minutes; remove from heat; let stand covered for 1 hour. Add marrow beef bones and beef shank slices; bring to boiling; simmer for 2 hours. Cool; remove meat and bones from beans; return lean meat to soup. Scoop marrow from bones; add to soup; discard bones. Mash half the beans by rubbing through a wire strainer, or whirl in blender with some of the liquid. Return to whole beans in pan. Next, prepare cooked vegetables. Heat 4 TBS. olive oil in a frying pan. Add diced onions; cook until soft. Add diced carrots, celery, and leeks; cook for 5 minutes over medium heat. Mix in tomatoes, mashing slightly. Simmer rapidly for 10 minutes or until most of liquid has evaporated. Add to prepared bean stock; simmer 30 minutes. Season with salt. To boiling soup, stir in diced potatoes and green beans. Simmer rapidly, uncovered, for 10 minutes; add sliced zucchini, shredded cabbage, and macaroni. Simmer 5 minutes more. In another pan, sauté the chopped parsley, minced garlic and dried basil in 2 TBS. olive oil until parsley is bright green. Mix into soup and serve. Sprinkle grated Parmesan cheese into each bowl. Makes 6-7 quarts.

Tuna Chowder

1/4 cup butter
1/2 cup celery, chopped
1 cup onion, chopped
1 cup potato, chopped
3 TBS. flour
3 cups milk
2 6-oz. cans tuna

1 cup Jack cheese, grated
1/2 tsp. thyme
1/2 tsp. dill
1 tsp. salt
1/2 tsp. pepper
1/4 cup parsley

Melt butter in a large skillet. Sauté vegetables about 3-5 minutes or until tender. Stir in flour until well blended. Gradually add milk. Cook over low heat until thick, stirring frequently. Add rest of ingredients and heat thoroughly. Serves 6.

Danny's Cheatin' Chili

1 can Campbell's Black Bean Soup
1 can black beans, drained
1 1/2 cups chunky salsa
1 lb. browned beef, turkey or pork
1 cup water

nonfat sour cream
scallions
cilantro
Jack cheese

Put first five ingredients in a pot and simmer over medium-low heat for 15 minutes. Garnish with nonfat sour cream, scallions, cheese and cilantro.

Front Nine Bean Soup Mix

Bean Mix
One pound each:
black beans
red beans
barley pearls
pinto beans
navy beans
great northern beans
split peas
dried lentils
black-eyed peas

Combine all ingredients, divide into ten 2-cup packages or jars for gift giving. The beans look pretty layered in glass containers. Pack with soup bowls or in a soup tureen. Include recipe for soup, as follows:

Nine Bean Soup

2 cups Nine Bean Soup Mix
2 quarts water
1 pound ham, diced
1 large onion, chopped
2 large cloves garlic, minced

1 1/2 tsp. salt
1 16-oz. can tomatoes
1 16-oz. can tomatoes and chilies
1/2 small jar mild picante sauce

Wash beans and put them in a pot covered with water (2 inches above beans) and soak overnight. Drain beans, add two quarts of water and next four ingredients. Cover and bring to a boil. Reduce heat and simmer one and one-half hours or until beans are tender. Add remaining ingredients and simmer one hour, stirring occasionally. Correct seasoning to taste.

Monday Nite Football Minestrone

Simmer covered for 10 minutes:
2 quarts chicken broth
3 med. potatoes in 1-inch cubes
1/2 lb. fresh green beans
3 carrots, sliced
1 med. onion, sliced
salt and pepper to taste

Add and simmer 10 minutes longer:
1/2 lb. zucchini, sliced
1 16-oz. can kidney beans, drained
pasta shells

Add this paste just before serving:
1 6-oz. can tomato paste
4 cloves squeezed garlic
1 TBS. basil
1/2 cup fresh Parmesan cheese
1/2 cup chopped parsley
1/4 cup olive oil

Stir together and serve in soup bowls. Serves 4-6.

Murphy's Law: If you keep your head down your score will be different...not better, just different.

Nikey's Lentil Soup

4 slices bacon, diced
1/2 lb. spicy Italian sausage
2 medium-sized onions, sliced
2 medium-sized carrots, sliced
1 large celery stalk, sliced
1 16-oz. pkg. dry lentils
1 bay leaf
8 cups water
1/2 tsp. pepper
1/2 tsp. thyme leaves
3/4 tsp. salt
2 TBS. lemon juice

Place Italian sausage in 5-quart Dutch Oven with 2 TBS. water, cover and cook 4 minutes over medium heat until water evaporates. Continue cooking 7 more minutes with lid off. Turn often. Remove, slice lengthwise once and then slice into bite-sized pieces. Set aside on a paper towel to absorb grease. Rinse pan. Cook bacon in same pan over low heat until lightly browned; push to side of Dutch oven. Add onions, carrots, and celery; over medium heat, cook until vegetables are tender. Add sausage, lentils, bay leaf, water, salt, pepper and thyme; over high heat, heat to boiling. Reduce heat to low; cover and simmer 1 hour or until lentils are tender. Discard bay leaf. Stir in lemon juice and adjust salt if needed. Serves 6.

To err is human and the Mulligan is divine. But laughter is still the best medicine on the golf course.

Lobster & Corn Chowder

4 oz. bacon, chopped
1 small onion, chopped
1 small green Bell pepper, chopped
1/3 cup all purpose flour
4 cups milk
1 cup heavy cream
4 ears of corn shucked, **or** 9 oz. frozen
nutmeg
mace
cayenne pepper
1/4 cup butter
salt and white pepper to taste
1 lb. (2 cups) shelled, cooked lobster meat

Fry bacon until crisp in large stockpot or heavy kettle. Remove bacon from pot and drain on paper towels. Remove most of bacon fat from pot; return bacon to pot. Add onion and green pepper; sauté for 5 minutes. Add flour to pot and blend well. Add milk and cream gradually, stirring constantly. Stir over medium-high heat until soup thickens, approximately 10 to 15 minutes. Cut kernels from corn ears with sharp knife and add to soup. Stir in nutmeg, mace, cayenne pepper and butter. Season soup with salt and white pepper. Add lobster to soup and simmer for 5 minutes. Serves 6.

 It takes 17 holes to really get warmed up.

Chilled Shrimp & Cucumber Soup

2 large cucumbers, peeled, seeded, chopped
1/4 cup red wine vinegar
1 TBS. sugar
1 tsp. salt
1 lb. small raw shrimp, peeled, deveined
2 TBS. unsalted butter
1/4 cup dry white vermouth
salt to taste
freshly ground black pepper to taste
1 1/2 cups buttermilk, chilled
3/4 cup chopped fresh dillweed
sprigs of fresh dillweed for garnish

Toss cucumbers with vinegar, sugar and salt and let stand for 30 minutes. Rinse shrimp and pat dry. Melt butter in small skillet, add shrimp and toss over medium-high heat until pink, about 2 minutes. Remove shrimp from skillet with slotted spoon and set aside in small bowl. Add vermouth to skillet and boil until reduced to a few spoonfuls. Pour reduced vermouth over shrimp and season with salt and pepper. Drain cucumber and transfer to food processor. Process cucumbers; add buttermilk and continue to process until smooth. Add dill and pulse once. Pour cucumber mixture into large bowl; add shrimp mixture and refrigerate, covered, until very cold. Serve in chilled bowls, garnished with sprigs of fresh dill. Serves 6.

Quick Southwestern Stew

1 lb. boned center loin pork chops, cubed
2 cups chopped yellow onions
4 minced cloves of garlic
1 tsp. dried oregano
1 1/2 TBS. New Mexico chili powder
3 14 1/2-oz. cans hominy, rinsed and drained
1 7-oz. can diced green chilies
5 cups low-sodium chicken broth
lime wedges
sliced green onions

In a 5-6 quart pan, stir pork, yellow onions, garlic and 1/3 cup broth. Cover tightly, bring to a boil over high heat, then simmer over medium heat for 10 minutes. Uncover, stir over medium-high heat until juices mostly stick to the pan and turn deep brown, about 4 minutes. Add 2 TBS. broth, stir until juices are well browned, about 4 minutes. Add oregano and chili powder and stir for 30 seconds. Stir in remaining broth, hominy and green chilies. Bring to a boil, reduce heat and simmer covered until well blended, about 10 minutes. Season to taste and serve with green onion and lime. Serves 4.

Law of Hazards: A new ball never carries over a lake.

Clam Chowder For 40

3 cups chopped onion
2 cups chopped celery
2 quarts diced potatoes
3 40-oz. cans chopped clams
3 bottles clam juice
salt and pepper
1/3 cup oil
1/2 lb. margarine
3 cups flour
1 gallon milk, scalded
2 cans evaporated milk
2 tsp. Worcestershire sauce
1/2 tsp. Tabasco
salt and pepper to taste (about 3 tsp. salt)
bacon, cooked and crumbled for topping

Cook until tender, onions, celery and potatoes in enough water to cover. Do not drain water. Add salt, pepper, clams and clam juice. In a separate sauce pan, make a roux with oil, margarine and flour. Gradually add hot scalded milk and evaporated milk, beating until smooth. Add Worcestershire and Tabasco. Combine all. To serve, heat, but do not boil and sprinkle crumbled cooked bacon on top. Invite the Club over.

Never putt a gimme.

Tomato Basil Chicken Stew

1 whole chicken, skinned
1 pkg. Knorr Tomato Basil Soup Mix
1 pkg. little white boiling onions
4 white potatoes, skinned
1 pkg. sliced mushrooms
6 carrots, sliced
2 large yellow onions, chopped
6 cloves fresh crushed garlic
1 14 1/2-oz. can stewed tomatoes, chopped
1 15 1/2-oz. can garbonzo beans
1 14 1/2-oz. can green beans
1 15 1/2-oz. can red kidney beans
6 stalks celery, chopped
Lawry's garlic salt

Boil the skinned chicken. Refrigerate overnight and remove fat. Sauté all vegetables with garlic salt. Combine package soup mix and liquids. Cook slowly over low heat all day.

*If you learn to **feel** the swing, you won't have to think so hard with your head.*

Bajamar Tortilla Soup

1 small onion, finely chopped
2-4 cloves garlic, minced
6 cups chicken broth
2 14-oz. cans chopped tomatoes
1 4-oz. can chopped green chilies
3 TBS. chopped fresh cilantro
1/2-1 tsp. ground cumin
salt, pepper to taste
1 tsp. sugar
juice of 2 limes
1/2-1 cup shredded cooked chicken breasts or 2 small boneless, skinless
uncooked breasts, chopped
1/2-1 cup shredded Monterey Jack cheese
1 cup broken tortilla chips, lightly salted
cilantro sprigs for garnish

In a 6-quart saucepan combine onion, garlic, and broth. Bring to a boil. Reduce heat and simmer 10 minutes. Add all remaining ingredients except cheese, tortilla chips and cilantro sprigs. Stir mixture well, cover and simmer about 30 minutes more. If liquid cooks down too much, add water to bring up to 8 cups. When ready to serve, warm bowls; bring soup almost to a boil. Put one heaping tablespoon of cheese and one handful of chips in each bowl. Fill bowls with very hot soup. Arrange several sprigs of cilantro on top of each bowl of soup for garnish. Serve immediately.

Pumpkin Soup

This is a wonderful low-fat recipe. A quick and easy fall soup.

1 16-oz. can chicken broth
1 1/2 cups unsweetened pumpkin puree
2/3 cup nonfat milk
1 tsp. sugar
1 tsp. ginger
pinch of cayenne pepper
pinch of salt
croutons

Place all ingredients in a saucepan. Simmer over low heat for 5-10 minutes.
Serve with croutons. Sprinkle with parsley. Serves 4.

Golf is a game in which you yell "fore", shoot six and write down five.

Black-Eyed Peas and Ribs

This dish is great when served with a green salad and French bread.

1 large onion, diced
2 cloves garlic
1 bay leaf
2 tsp. salt
sage
coarsely ground black pepper
salt
1 bottle Burgundy wine
6 spareribs
4 cans black-eyed peas, drained

Place the ribs and black-eyed peas in a Dutch oven. Add a large diced onion, garlic cloves, bay leaf, a pinch of sage, some black pepper and 2 tsp. of salt. Last add 1 bottle of Burgundy wine (yes, one whole bottle). Simmer until peas and ribs are tender (about 4 hours). Serves 6.

Always carry two putters in your golf bag. You never know when you might want to break one.

Artichoke Leek Soup

3 med. leeks
1 TBS. olive oil
2 med. cloves garlic, peeled, minced
2 TBS. white rice
1 large baking potato, peeled, coarsely chopped
1 14-oz. can artichoke hearts, drained, halved
4 cups chicken broth
3/4 tsp. ground cumin
1/4 tsp. dried thyme, crumbled
1/8 tsp. cayenne pepper
freshly ground black pepper to taste
1 TBS. lemon juice
1 TBS. finely chopped parsley or minced chives

Cut all but 2 inches of the dark green from the tops of the leeks. Split leeks down the center and wash well under cold running water to remove the grit. Slice thin. In a medium pan heat the oil over medium heat. Add the leeks and garlic; sauté 5 minutes. Stir in the rice and sauté 3 minutes. Add the potato, artichokes, broth, cumin, thyme and cayenne. Bring to a boil; reduce the heat to medium-low, cover and simmer 30 minutes. Let soup cool a few minutes before pureeing in several batches in a food processor or blender. Pour back into the pan and season with several grindings black pepper, lemon juice, parsley or chives. Heat through. Garnish with a few croutons and parsley or chives. Serves 4.

The Law of the Tee: One must always know when one is teed up and one is teed off.

Chili Non Carne

3/4 cup chopped onion
2 cloves garlic, minced
3 TBS. olive oil
3 TBS. chili powder
1/4 tsp. basil
1/4 tsp. oregano
1/4 tsp. cumin
2 cups finely chopped zucchini
1 cup finely chopped carrot
1 28-oz. can tomatoes, drained, diced
1 14-oz. can tomatoes, drained, diced
1 15-oz. can kidney beans, undrained
2 15-oz. cans kidney beans, drained and thoroughly rinsed
chopped onions, tomatoes, lettuce, or green peppers, for garnish

In a large pot, sauté onion and garlic in olive oil until soft. Mix in chili powder, basil, oregano, and cumin. Stir in zucchini and carrots until well blended. Cook for about 1 minute over low heat, stirring occasionally. Stir in chopped tomatoes, undrained kidney beans, and drained kidney beans. Bring to a boil. Reduce heat and simmer for 30-45 minutes or until thick. Top with chopped onions, tomatoes, and lettuce and/or green peppers. Serves 8.

On The Green
Salads & Dressings

On The Green - Salads and Dressings

Dilled Yogurt Dressing

1 cup low fat yogurt
2 TBS. vinegar
1/2 tsp. dill seeds
1/2 small onion, chopped
1/4 tsp. dry mustard
1/2 clove garlic, minced.

Mix all ingredients together and chill in refrigerator.

Bill's Salad Dressing

1/2 cup olive oil
1/2 cup salad oil
1/2 cup cider vinegar
1 clove garlic, pressed
1/2 tsp. dry mustard
salt and freshly ground pepper

Shake vigorously to blend. Store in refrigerator.

It's important to get a feel for your clubs. Never buy one until you've thrown it.

BoBo's Broccoli Salad

Contributed by Kay McMahon
LPGA & PGA
Teaching Professional

Once served to a group of professional golfers and friends. All too polite to say they did not much care for broccoli. But in the McMahon tradition...Try it, you might like it. Try it they did...All went back for thirds with the only remaining instruction for this famous dish being to pass on the recipe. Dedicated to my family and friends and their true loves...golf, cooking and eating. Broccoli and birdies to all! Kay

4-6 stalks broccoli (raw; use stalks, too)
12-16 strips bacon, browned, crumbled
1 cup raisins
1 bunch green onions **or** 1 red onion (optional)
3/4 cup mayonnaise
1 1/2 TBS. sugar
1 1/2 TBS. red wine vinegar

Chop broccoli and onions into small pieces. Mix ingredients. Refrigerate until ready to serve. Best if made a day ahead.

 "Learning to eat does not always make one a cook...Just as playing golf does not always make one a teacher. Therefore, when accepting golf advice, take it with a grain of salt. Too much salt always spoils the gravy." Kay McMahon, 1995 LPGA National Teacher of the Year.

Tabbouleh (Bulgar Salad)

It's easy to peel tomatoes if they are immersed in boiling water for a few seconds.

1/2 cup bulgar
1/2 cup fresh mint, minced
2 cups peeled tomatoes, chopped
1/2 tsp. salt
1/3 cup olive oil
1/2 cup green onions, minced
1 cup fresh parsley
1/3 cup lemon juice
1/4 tsp. black pepper
Romaine lettuce leaves

Soak bulgar in cold water (about 45 minutes) until tender. Drain and squeeze as dry as possible in clean tea towel or by pressing bulgar against a sieve with the back of a spoon. Place drained bulgar in a bowl and add green onions, parsley, mint, and tomatoes. Stir in lemon juice, salt and pepper. Let stand about 30 minutes to allow flavors to blend. Stir in oil. Put mixture in a bowl and surround with inside leaves of Romaine to use for scooping.

The force of attraction between a golf ball and a sandtrap increases with the need for a birdie.

Summer Barley Salad

2 cups barley, rinsed and drained
4 cups chicken broth
2 cups thinly sliced celery
1 cup thinly sliced green onions
1 5-oz. can sliced water chestnuts, drained
1 TBS. grated orange peel
3/4 cup orange juice
2 TBS. lemon juice
2 TBS. sweet-hot mustard
1/4 tsp. nutmeg
1 cup nonfat plain yogurt
lettuce for garnish

In a 3 to 4-quart pan, bring barley and broth to a boil over a high heat. Cover and simmer over a low heat until barley is tender to the bite (about 30 minutes). Let cool. Mix barley with celery, green onions and water chestnuts. If making ahead, cover and chill. Combine orange peel, orange juice, lemon juice, mustard and nutmeg; stir this mixture into the yogurt. Add yogurt dressing to barley just prior to serving. Mound on a platter garnished with lettuce. Serves 8-10.

Drive for show...putt for dough.

Pomegranate and Endive Salad

In this recipe pears can be substituted for pomegranates if not in season.

6 small handfuls watercress
6 handfuls Belgian endive
3/4 cup walnut **or** extra virgin olive oil
6 TBS. raspberry **or** red wine vinegar
salt and freshly ground black pepper to taste
6 TBS. pomegranate seeds
6 TBS. chopped walnuts, lightly toasted

Arrange the watercress on each salad plate. Arrange the larger leaves of endive to resemble fingers across the watercress. In a small bowl, whisk together oil and vinegar, seasoning to taste with salt and pepper. Drizzle the dressing over the greens, then scatter pomegranate seeds and walnuts on top.

Filled Avocados

4 ripe avocados   mayonnaise
6 hard boiled eggs   Tabasco
1 lb. cooked and shelled shrimp   chopped parsley

Cut avocados in half lengthwise and remove stone. Scoop out a little of the center and mix with half of the shrimp, mayonnaise, chopped egg whites, and Tabasco to taste. Reserve the egg yolks for garnishing. Fill the avocados with the shrimp mixture and garnish with remaining shrimp and sieved egg yolks and chopped parsley. Serves 8.

Raspberry Vinaigrette Salad

This dressing is good on salad, fruit, or grilled boneless chicken breasts.

Salad
1 cup torn Romaine lettuce
1 cup torn green leaf lettuce
1 cup torn Butter or Boston lettuce
1 8 1/2-oz. can artichoke hearts, halved
1/2 cup walnuts, chopped

Dressing
1/3 cup canola oil
3 TBS. sugar
2 TBS. raspberry vinegar
1 TBS. sour cream
1 1/2 tsp. Dijon mustard
1/2 cup fresh or frozen whole raspberries

In a small bowl, combine all dressing ingredients except raspberries; blend well using wire whisk. Fold in raspberries. Refrigerate at least one hour to blend flavors. Arrange all salad ingredients except walnuts on 4-6 individual chilled salad plates. Drizzle dressing over salad; sprinkle with walnuts. Garnish with fresh raspberries if desired. Can substitute nonfat sour cream. Serves 4-6.

Paella Salad

3 TBS. olive oil
3 large garlic cloves, minced
1 small onion, finely chopped
2 cups long grain rice
4 1/2 cups chicken broth
1 tsp. saffron threads, crumbled
1/4 tsp. turmeric
1/2 tsp. dried thyme
1 whole cooked chicken breast, skinned, boned, cut into bite-sized pieces

12 medium-sized cooked shrimp, shelled, deveined
1/2 lb. cooked chorizo
1 large sweet red pepper, seeded, diced
1 large ripe tomato
14 oz. can artichoke hearts, drained and sliced
1 cup frozen peas
6 large green onions, chopped
1/2 cup fresh parsley, chopped
14 olives (Kalamata), pitted, halved

Heat oil in a heavy sauce pan. Add garlic and onion and cook until tender, about 2 minutes. Add rice and stir to coat with oil. Add broth, saffron, turmeric and thyme. Cover and bring to a boil. Reduce heat and simmer until water is absorbed, about 25 minutes. Transfer rice to a large bowl and cool to room temperature. Add chicken, shrimp, chorizo, red pepper, tomato, artichoke hearts, peas, green onions, parsley, and olives to rice. Stir to combine, then add enough vinaigrette to lightly coat ingredients. Stir gently, taste and adjust seasonings if necessary. Refrigerate until serving.
Serves 10-12.

Dressing

2/3 cup olive oil
2 TBS. red wine vinegar
1/4 cup fresh lemon juice

1 large garlic clove, minced
1/4 cup finely chopped fresh parsley
salt and lots of freshly ground pepper

Combine oil, vinegar, lemon juice, garlic, parsley, salt and pepper in a small bowl.

Sunshine Salad

2 pkgs. gelatin
1/2 cup cold orange juice
1 cup heated orange juice
1/4 cup sugar
1/8 tsp. salt
1/4 cup lemon juice
1 cup grated carrots
1 8-oz. can crushed pineapple

In a blender, sprinkle gelatin over cold juice and let stand 4 minutes. Add hot juice and process at low speed about 2 minutes. Add sugar, salt and lemon juice; process at high speed until blended. Add grated carrots. Blend again. Pour into 8-inch baking pan and stir in pineapple and chill until firm. Serves 6.

Bev's Broccoli Salad

1 red onion, finely chopped
1 bunch fresh broccoli, finely chopped
3-4 ripe tomatoes, finely chopped
1 can kidney beans, drained
1 bottle Italian dressing
Tabasco, to taste
grated Cheddar cheese

Toss first 6 ingredients in a bowl. Marinate overnight. Add grated cheese before serving.

Real McCoy Salad

2 small pkgs. lemon Jell-O
3 1/4 cups boiling water
14 marshmallows, diced

4 bananas, sliced
2 lb. can crushed pineapple, drained, juice reserved for topping

Mix Jell-O and water. Cool. Add marshmallows, bananas, and pineapple.

Topping
pineapple juice
1 egg
1/2 cup sugar

1 tsp. flour
1 cup sour cream
Cheddar cheese

Cook together 1 cup pineapple juice, 1 egg, 1/2 cup sugar and 1 tsp. flour; cool. Add 1 cup sour cream and mix well. Spread over top of salad and cover with grated Cheddar cheese.

Jean's Curried Chicken Salad

1/2 cup plain yogurt
1/2 cup mayonnaise
1 TBS. freshly squeezed lemon juice
2 TBS. hot or mild curry powder to taste
1/4 cup cashews, toasted, chopped
6 boneless chicken breasts, skinless
1 cup finely chopped unpeeled apple
1/4 cup finely chopped sweet pickle
1/2 cup dried raisins or currants, plumped in hot water for 15 minutes and drained
2 TBS. minced green onions including some green tops
fresh minced parsley, preferably flat-leaf type for garnish

In a small bowl, combine the yogurt, mayonnaise, lemon juice and curry powder. Blend well and set aside. Toast the nuts, chop coarsely and set aside. Boil chicken breasts until done; cut into cubes. In a larger bowl, combine the chicken, apple, pickle, drained raisins or currants, onion and toasted nuts. Stir in the yogurt dressing to taste. Transfer to a serving bowl or serve on individual plates over bed of lettuce and sprinkle with parsley.

"For most amateurs, the best wood in the bag is the pencil."
Chi Chi Rodriguez.

Chinese Chicken Salad

4-5 stalks green onion
4 TBS. sesame seeds, browned in a dry pan over medium heat
3-4 chicken breasts
fresh ginger
1 medium head cabbage
4 oz. slivered almonds, browned in a dry pan over medium heat
2 pkgs. Top Ramen Noodles, sesame flavored

Simmer chicken in water, ginger and white wine. When chicken is done remove from liquid and cool. Shred cooled chicken into pieces. Quarter cabbage and slice into thin strips. Chop green onions diagonally into small pieces. Brown sesame seeds and almonds in a small pan over medium heat, stirring constantly. Mix cabbage, noodles and chicken. Add chopped onions, sesame seeds and nuts. Toss with dressing and chill. Serves 6.

Dressing

1 TBS. sesame oil	1/2 cup vegetable oil
7 TBS. rice vinegar	4 TBS. sugar
2 tsp. salt	1 tsp. black pepper

Mix well to blend.

When deciding where to place your approach shot remember, they never move the middle of the green.

Chicken-Rice Salad with Artichokes

1/4 tsp. celery seed
1 clove garlic, minced
1 scallion, finely chopped
1/8 tsp. sugar
1/4 cup fresh parsley, chopped
1 TBS. red wine vinegar
3 TBS. olive oil
1 6-oz. jar marinated artichokes, roughly diced
1/2 4-oz. jar pimientos, chopped
1 celery stalk, thinly sliced
1/2 small green Bell pepper, chopped
salt, pepper

In medium bowl, combine celery seed, garlic, scallions, sugar, parsley, vinegar, and oil. Blend well. Add artichokes (including marinade), pimientos, celery and green Bell pepper. Coat well and marinate overnight.

Salad
3/4 cup Basmati rice (can use wild rice)
2 whole chicken breasts, cooked and diced
1/3 cup mayonnaise
6 oz. mushrooms, sliced
lettuce

Using 1 1/2 cups of water or chicken broth, cook rice for 20 minutes or according to package. Combine rice, chicken and mayonnaise. Add sliced mushrooms and marinated mixture. Correct seasoning. Stir and chill. Serve on lettuce cups.

Jicama & Orange Chicken Salad with Cilantro

4 1/2 cups cubed cooked chicken breasts
4 1/2 cups cubed or julienned jicama
2 TBS. lemon juice
1/4 cup orange juice
1/4 cup honey
1 garlic clove, minced
1/4 cup oil
1/2 tsp. pepper
1/2 tsp salt
2 11-oz. cans mandarin oranges, drained **or** fresh oranges
2-4 TBS. snipped fresh cilantro leaves

Combine chicken and jicama in a bowl. Combine the lemon juice, orange juice, honey, garlic, oil, pepper and salt and mix well; add to chicken and jicama. Chill mixture several hours or overnight. Before serving add oranges and cilantro. Serves 10.

Is my friend in the bunker or is the "★!☺⚏?" on the green?

Mexican Salad Grande

Salad Grande is easy and delicious and it feeds a crowd.

2 or 3 large tomatoes, cut in wedges
2 red onions, cut in rings and then halved
2 6-oz. cans black olives, sliced
2 heads Romaine lettuce, broken in pieces
2 heads Iceberg lettuce, broken in pieces
2 cups shredded Cheddar cheese
2 large California avocados, sliced
2 6-oz. bags corn chips
2 15-oz. cans kidney beans, well drained
2 15-oz. cans Garbonzo beans, well drained
salt and pepper to taste
salsa

Toss all ingredients except corn chips and salsa with Grey Poupon Dressing. Just before serving toss with chips and serve with a side of salsa.

Grey Poupon Dressing
1 tsp. salt
1 tsp. sugar
2/3 cup cider vinegar
1 1/3 cups olive oil
2 tsp. Grey Poupon mustard

Mix well and let sit for 1 hour before tossing salad.

Cranberry Mold

2 cups coarsely chopped fresh cranberries
2 cups sugar
6 oz. lemon-flavored gelatin
2 cups hot water
2 cups canned crushed pineapple, drained, reserving syrup
2 cups syrup from canned pineapple
2 cups chopped celery
1 cup broken walnuts

Combine cranberries and sugar. In large bowl dissolve gelatin in hot water. Add pineapple syrup to gelatin. Mix well; chill until partially set. Add cranberry mixture, pineapple, celery and walnuts. Pour into 2-quart melon mold, chill until firm. Unmold onto serving platter. Garnish as desired. Beautiful on a holiday table, garnished with fresh flowers and/or orange slices.

If players are hitting golf balls into your face, you're probably on the wrong fairway.

Layered Pasta Salad

1 1/2 cups uncooked small shell macaroni
1 TBS. vegetable oil
1 cup shredded ham
1 10-oz. pkg. frozen petite peas, thawed
1 cup shredded Monterey Jack cheese
1/2 cup sour cream
1/2 cup sliced green onions
2 cups shredded lettuce
3 hard cooked eggs, sliced
2 tsp. Dijon mustard
1/2 cup mayonnaise
1/2 tsp. salt
1/8 tsp. pepper

Cook macaroni, drain and rinse with cold water. Combine macaroni and oil. Toss to coat lightly. Layer lettuce, macaroni, ham, egg slices, peas and cheese. Combine mayonnaise and remaining ingredients and mix well. Spread mixture over salad and seal with plastic wrap. Chill 12 hours or overnight. Toss gently before serving. Serves 8-10.

Murphy's Law of Improvement: Any correction made to your swing works......once.

The Vintage Club's "Heart Throb" Tuna Salad

Salad
16 oz. solid white tuna (water packed), drained
1/3 cup apple (skin on), finely diced, dipped in rice wine vinegar and drained
1/3 cup red pepper, finely diced
1/3 cup yellow pepper, finely diced
1/3 cup carrot, finely diced
1/3 cup celery, finely diced
2 TBS. fresh dill, chopped (optional)

Flake tuna in mixing bowl. Add other salad ingredients to tuna and mix. Add Apple Cider Dressing and mix. Chill until ready to serve. Display as a salad mold for a buffet or make individual servings. Garnish with fresh colorful vegetables, a fresh dill sprig and a slice of fruit nut bread. Serves 4-8.

Apple Cider Dressing
1/2 cup apple cider or apple juice
1/3 cup rice wine vinegar
1 1/2 TBS. sugar (optional) **or** sugar substitute to taste
2 1/2 TBS. Dijon mustard (optional)

Mix all apple cider dressing ingredients together and hold.

Never trust an 18 handicapper who carries a one-iron in his bag.

Lentil Salad with Mint and Feta

1 1/2 cups lentils
3 TBS. olive oil
3 TBS. red wine vinegar
3 TBS. finely chopped fresh mint
1 garlic clove, minced
2 tomatoes, chopped, seeded
1 small yellow Bell pepper
2 green onions, sliced
7 oz. Feta cheese, crumbled

Place lentils in a saucepan. Cover with 4 inches of water. Season water with salt. Boil until just tender, about 25 minutes. Drain; cool slightly. Combine oil and vinegar, mint and garlic in a large bowl. Add warm lentils; toss. Refrigerate until well chilled. (Lentils can be prepared 1 day ahead.) Add tomatoes, Bell pepper and green onions to lentils. Season to taste with salt and pepper. Divide salad among plates. Sprinkle Feta over lentils.

Golf is 50% mental....90% of the time.

Layered Spinach Salad

1 lb. spinach
1/2 lb. bacon
1 box frozen peas
1/2 head lettuce

1 sliced red onion, soaked in cold water for
30 minutes with 3 TBS. sugar
2 cups mayonnaise
1 cup sour cream
Swiss cheese, grated

Wash, dry, and tear spinach. Sprinkle with salt, pepper and sugar. Add crumbled bacon (11 slices) and sliced eggs. Tear 1/2 head lettuce; mix with spinach. Layer peas and red onion. Mix 2 cups of mayonnaise and 1 cup sour cream; layer. Seal bowl with plastic wrap and refrigerate. Before serving, toss and sprinkle with grated white Swiss cheese. Serves 12.

Corn and Pepper Salad

1 can whole kernel corn, drained (or use fresh or frozen)
1/2 green pepper, chopped
1/2 red pepper, chopped
1 Spanish onion, sliced in rings
1 bunch watercress

Dressing
6 TBS. salad oil
2 TBS. wine vinegar
salt, ground pepper

2 TBS. chopped parsley
pinch sugar

Mix veggies together and toss with dressing.

Strawberry Jell-O Salad

1 large strawberry or cherry Jell-O
1 cup boiling water
1 TBS. lemon juice
1 14 1/2-oz. can crushed pineapple
1 container frozen strawberries, partially thawed
1 half pint of sour cream

Dissolve Jell-O in 1 cup boiling water; stir until completely dissolved. Add 1 tsp. lemon juice, crushed pineapple and container of frozen strawberries. Put half of above mixture in 9 x 11 x 2-inch baking dish and put in the refrigerator to set Jell-O. Stir sour cream with a spoon until smooth and easy to spread and spread with spoonfuls on the Jell-O. Layer and spread with back of spoon. Spread the remaining Jell-O mixture on top of the sour cream and return to the refrigerator. Cover with plastic wrap until time to serve. It can be made the day before. Cut into squares. Serves 6-8. Doubled this will serve 16; use 11" x 13" glass dish. It will be slightly thicker.

"It's hard to recover from a great drive."

Southwestern Pasta Salad

1 16-oz. pkg. penne or mostaccioli pasta, uncooked
Creamy Southwestern Salad Dressing
lettuce leaves
1 15-oz. can black beans, rinsed and drained
1 cup frozen whole kernel corn
1 sweet red pepper, chopped
4 green onions, sliced
1/3 cup chopped fresh cilantro
fresh cilantro sprigs

Cook pasta according to package directions; drain. Rinse with cold water and drain. Combine pasta and 1 3/4 cups dressing; toss gently. Chill. Spoon pasta mixture onto a lettuce lined serving platter. Top with black beans and next 4 ingredients. Garnish, if desired. Serve with remaining dressing. Serves 6.

Creamy Southwestern Salad Dressing
1 8-oz. carton nonfat sour cream
1 16-oz. jar mild thick and chunky salsa
1/2 tsp. ground cumin
2 cloves garlic, minced

Combine all ingredients; chill. Yields 2 3/4 cups.

Strawberry & Onion Salad with Poppy Seed Dressing

Salad
1 head Romaine lettuce
1 pint fresh strawberries
1 Bermuda onion, sliced

Wash Romaine lettuce. Place greens on individual salad plates, or in large salad bowl. Slice strawberries. Put berries and onions on top of greens. Drizzle poppy seed dressing over salad. Toss, if using large salad bowl. Serves 8.

Dressing
1/2 cup mayonnaise
2 TBS. vinegar
1/3 cup sugar
1/4 cup whole milk
2 TBS. poppy seeds

Place all ingredients in a jar. Cover and shake until blended. Dressing keeps several days in refrigerator.

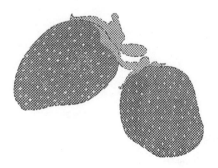

Nonfat Mustard Salad Dressing

1/2 cup nonfat yogurt
2 TBS. Dijon mustard
1 TBS. capers
4-5 cloves roasted garlic
1/2 cup dry white wine
1 TBS. dried thyme (can use oregano or basil or cilantro)
2 TBS. lemon juice
2 TBS. Balsamic vinegar

Emulsify all ingredients in a food processor.

Berry Patch Salad

Salad
1 med. red onion, sliced in rings
1 small head Butter lettuce
1 quart fresh strawberries or grapes

Celery Seed Dressing

1/2 cup sugar	1 tsp. salt
1/2 cup oil	1 tsp. celery seed
1/4 cup white vinegar	1 tsp. mustard

Pour a little boiling water over sliced onions. Drain. Add berries and onions to lettuce and toss with dressing.

Grilled Chicken on Greens

Salad
1 10-oz. bag fresh spinach, torn
1 head Boston lettuce, torn
1 head Romaine lettuce, torn
1 can mandarin oranges
4 oz. peanuts
1 box cherry tomatoes
1 red onion, sliced
5 chicken breasts, grilled and diced
whole pecans
red grapes, halved

Combine all ingredients for salad. Toss with dressing. Serves 10-15.

Dressing
1/2 cup lemon juice
2 TBS. Dijon mustard
2 tsp. salt
1 1/2 tsp. cayenne pepper
1 cup honey
3/4 cup olive oil
3/4 cup canola oil
5 tsp. poppy seeds

Combine all ingredients and process in a blender.

Lancer's Restaurant Famous Salad Dressing

Lancer's Restaurant was on a rocky hill on Mt. Rose and very popular. It burned to the ground in the 1960's and was never rebuilt.

1 1/2 tsp. salt
1 1/2 tsp. sugar
1 1/2 tsp. dry mustard
1/4 tsp. garlic powder **or** 1 clove fresh garlic, minced
1 tsp. crushed black pepper
1 TBS. Worcestershire sauce
1 1/2 tsp. A-1 steak sauce
1/4 cup Burgundy
1/4 cup ketchup
1/4 cup wine vinegar
1/4 cup honey
3/4 cup salad oil

Shake above ingredients in a quart jar then add 1/2 cup more salad oil. Lancer's served this dressing over spinach sprinkled with crushed bacon bits and chopped hard boiled eggs. Dressing is good on any salad greens. Yields one pint of dressing.

No putt ever got longer as a result of a ball being marked.

Tomato Aspic

Aspic
1 envelope unflavored gelatin
1/2 cup tomato juice, chilled
1 cup tomato juice, heated
1/4 cup chili sauce
1/2 cup celery, finely chopped
1/2 cup green onions, finely chopped
1/2 cup green Bell pepper, finely chopped
1 TBS. lemon juice
salt and pepper to taste

Soak gelatin in chilled tomato juice for five minutes. Add heated tomato juice to gelatin mixture and stir until gelatin is dissolved. Stir in remaining ingredients. Lightly spray individual molds with non-stick cooking spray and divide mixture evenly among the molds. Chill for several hours until set and then unmold onto lettuce leaves. Garnish with one teaspoon of the following dressing. Serves 6.

Dressing
2 level TBS. mayonnaise (use measuring spoon, not flatware)
1 TBS. lemon juice
1/8 tsp. horseradish
salt and paprika to taste (the paprika will give the dressing a nice pink color)

Mix and chill until needed for garnish.

Note: Do not use tomato juice from concentrate; it may be too thin.

Never leave a birdie putt short.

Cashew Sesame Noodle Salad

This dish can also be served warm as a side dish.

2 large garlic cloves, chopped
3 TBS. soy sauce
1 1/2 TBS. rice vinegar
1/4 cup Asian sesame oil
3/4 tsp. dried hot red pepper flakes, or to taste
1 tsp. sugar
1/2 cup salted roasted cashews
1/3 cup water
1 lb. thin spaghetti
1 1/2 cups loosely packed fresh coriander sprigs, chopped fine
cashews and coriander sprigs for garnish

In a blender whirl first 8 ingredients with salt and pepper to taste until
smooth. Sauce may be made 3 days ahead and chilled, covered. Bring
sauce to room temperature and stir before using. Cook spaghetti until
al dente. In a colander drain spaghetti and rinse well under cold water. In a
bowl toss with sauce and chopped coriander. Garnish sesame noodles with
cashews and coriander. Serves 4 as a salad.

The good player's head always stays behind the ball.

Honey Mustard Dressing

1 cup honey
2 cups mayonnaise (can use lite mayo)
1 1/2 cups prepared French's mustard
1/2 cup Grey Poupon mustard
1/8 cup dill weed

Place all ingredients in a small bowl and mix well. Keeps in refrigerator in covered jar for weeks.

Jutta's Sweet 'n Simple Coleslaw

1 head white cabbage, shredded
1 small green Bell pepper, sliced in thin rings
2 yellow onions, sliced in thin rings
3/4 cup sugar, plus 1 TBS.
1 tsp. dry mustard powder
1 tsp. celery seed
1 TBS. salt
1 cup white vinegar
3/4 cup vegetable oil

In a large bowl layer cabbage, green pepper and onion; sprinkle 3/4 cup sugar over all. In a saucepan combine remaining 1 TBS. sugar and other ingredients; mix well and heat to boiling. Pour over slaw; cover with plastic film or foil and refrigerate for at least 4 hours, or preferably overnight. Just before serving toss slaw. Will keep in refrigerator for 10 days or longer. Serves 8.

Kayser's Shrimp, Cantaloupe and Avocado Salad

1 head Bibb lettuce
1 small head red leaf lettuce
1/2 lb. spinach, washed, dried, and stemmed
1/2 lb. snow peas **or** sugar snap peas, trimmed, blanched and chilled
1 small cantaloupe
1 large ripe, firm avocado, peeled, seeded and sliced
1 1/2 lbs. shrimp
juice of 1 lemon
1/2 cup prepared chili sauce
1/3 cup honey
1 TBS. Worcestershire sauce
1 TBS. minced shallot
1/2 cup extra virgin olive oil
salt and freshly ground pepper to taste

Combine the juice of 1 lemon with the chili sauce, honey, Worcestershire, shallot and olive oil. Whisk well and set aside in refrigerator to chill if done ahead. Peel and devein the shrimp. Steam or grill on a well-oiled grill until just done. Toss while warm with 1/4 cup of the dressing and chill well. Tear lettuces and spinach into bite-sized pieces. Arrange in a large salad bowl. Peel and seed the cantaloupe, slice into strips approximately 1 x 3 x 1/2". Arrange decoratively over greens. Then arrange snow peas and chilled shrimp. Top with avocado slices and drizzle with dressing. Pass remaining dressing.

Murphy's Tee Shot Law: A brilliant tee shot means a three-putt green.

In The Cup

Sweets & Desserts

In The Cup - Sweets & Desserts

In The Cup - **Sweets & Desserts,** continued

The Famous Clipper's Chocolate Chip Cookies

1 cup butter, softened
3/4 cup sugar
3/4 cup light brown sugar, packed
1 TBS. vanilla
1 TBS. Tia Maria
1 TBS. Frangelico
2 eggs
1 tsp. baking soda
1/2 tsp. salt
2 1/2 cups all purpose flour
4 cups milk chocolate chips
1/2 cup walnut halves
1/2 cup pecan pieces
1/2 cup Macadamia nuts

Cream butter, sugars, vanilla, Tia Maria and Frangelico until light and fluffy. Add eggs; beat well. In another bowl combine flour, baking soda and salt; gradually beat into creamed mixture. Stir in chocolate chips and nuts. Mix well. Place in storage container and refrigerate overnight. Drop by teaspoonful onto ungreased cookie sheet. Bake at 325º for 10-13 minutes or until golden brown. Cool slightly and serve immediately. Makes 3-4 dozen.

Hale Irwin's Pecan Pie

Contributed by
Hale Irwin
PGA Professional

1 9-inch pie crust, unbaked
3 eggs
1/2 cup sugar
pinch salt
1 tsp. vanilla
1 cup dark Karo syrup
3 TBS. melted butter (not hot)
1 1/3-1 1/2 cups whole pecans (smallish)

Beat eggs with fork. Add rest of ingredients and mix well. Pour in shell and bake at 350º for 1/2 + hour. Do not bake over 3/4 hour. Pie must be set. Bake it closer to bottom of oven. Cool on rack. Serve with sweetened whipped cream (the real thing).

"Use one more club than normal and swing 80% of maximum for better contact and control." Hale Irwin

Katie Peterson-Parker's Pecan Glazes

Contributed by
Katie Peterson-Parker
LPGA Professional

1 lb. pecan halves
2 egg whites
1 cup sugar

4 TBS. cinnamon
1 tsp. ground cloves
1 tsp. nutmeg

Mix pecans in egg whites to coat. Roll coated pecans individually in sugar and spices which have been mixed together. Place pecans on ungreased cookie sheet and bake 10-12 minutes at 350º. Great for holidays!

Katie Peterson-Parker's Chocolate Caramel Bars

Contributed by
Katie Peterson-Parker
LPGA Professional

1 14-oz. bag Kraft caramels
2/3 cup (5 1/3-oz. can) evaporated milk
1 two-layer German chocolate cake mix with pudding
1/2 cup margarine, melted
1 1/2 cups chopped walnuts
1 6-oz. pkg. semi-sweet chocolate pieces

Melt caramels with 1/3 cup milk over low heat, stirring until smooth. Mix separately remaining milk, cake mix and margarine; mix well. Press half of cake mixture into bottom of greased 13x9-inch baking pan. Bake at 350º for 6 minutes. Sprinkle 1 cup walnuts and chocolate pieces over crust; top with caramel mixture spreading to edges of pan. Top with teaspoons of remaining cake mixture pressed gently into caramel mixture. Sprinkle with remaining walnuts, pressing lightly into top. Bake at 350º for 20 minutes. Cool slightly; refrigerate. Makes 2 dozen.

Ellie Gibson's
Chocolate Chip & Putt Cookies

Contributed by
Ellie Gibson
LPGA Professional

1 1/2 cups brown sugar
1 1/2 cups white sugar
2 cups shortening
2 eggs
4 1/2 cups flour

2 tsps. baking soda
2 tsps. salt
2 tsps. vanilla
1 cup walnuts or pecans
1 cup chocolate chips

ROUND 1: Combine and cream together:
brown sugar
white sugar
shortening
Add 2 eggs
Set aside!

ROUND 2: Combine in separate bowl:
flour
baking soda
salt

ROUND 3: Combine Round 1 and Round 2 in three stages; add 1 tsp. warm water between stages (total of 2 tsp. water). Add 2 tsp. vanilla to mixture. Add chopped walnuts or pecans and chocolate chips. Drop on sheet (about a golf ball size) and bake at 375° for 13-15 minutes.

"When chipping, always let your hands lead the way! Grip the club firmly and swing in a pendulum motion with very little wrist action. Hands firm and leading the entire way." Ellie Gibson

Tom Weiskopf's
Peasant Strawberry Tart

Contributed by
Tom Weiskopf
PGA Professional

This is a favorite recipe of Tom and Jeanne Weiskopf. It is a beautiful presentation recipe and easy too! Large spring berries are the prettiest.

Tart
1 1/3 cups all purpose flour
3 TBS. sugar
1/2 tsp. cardamom (optional and expensive, but well worth it)
1/2 cup butter, cut into pieces
1 egg yolk

Combine flour, sugar and cardamom with butter. Whirl in food processor or rub with fingers until coarse crumbs form. Blend in 1 egg yolk until dough sticks together. Press dough over the bottom and sides of an 11-inch tart pan with removable bottom. Bake in a 300º oven until golden, about 30 minutes.

Filling
6 cups strawberries, washed and hulled
3/4 cup quince **or** apple jelly
whipped cream

Arrange strawberries over baked crust so that point side faces up. In a small pan over low heat stir jelly until smooth and liquid. Spoon evenly over berries. Remove pan rim; cut tart into wedges. Whipped cream may be added before serving. Note: holds well in refrigerator for at least 2 hours.

"Golf is a good walk spoiled." Mark Twain

White Chocolate Macadamia Nut Cookies

1 1/2 cups butter
1 2/3 cups sugar
1 cup plus 2 TBS. brown sugar
3 eggs
2 tsp. vanilla
2 3/4 cups unsifted flour

3/4 tsp. baking powder
1 1/2 tsp. baking soda
1/2 tsp. salt
2 cups rolled oats
6 oz. white chocolate chips
1 cup macadamia nuts, chopped

Cream butter and sugars. Add eggs and vanilla; beat until light and fluffy. Sift together flour, baking powder, soda and salt. Blend into creamed mixture. Add rolled oats and chocolate chips. Drop by teaspoonful onto greased cookie sheet. Bake in 375º oven for 10-12 minutes. Yields 6 dozen.

Rhubarb Dream Dessert

1 cup flour
5 TBS. powdered sugar
1/2 cup butter or margarine (can use reduced fat margarine)

Blend above ingredients and press into ungreased 7x11-inch pan. Bake at 350º for 15 minutes.

2 beaten eggs
1 1/2 cups sugar
1/4 cup flour

1/2 tsp. salt
2 cups finely chopped rhubarb

Spoon above mixture over crust and continue baking at 350º for 35 minutes. Good served with whipped cream, ice cream or Cool Whip.

Lemon Torte with Raspberries

nonstick cooking spray
1 4-serving-size pkg. low-calorie lemon-flavored gelatin
1/2 cup boiling water
1/2 6-oz. can (1/3 cup) frozen lemonade concentrate, thawed
1 12-oz. can evaporated skim milk
2 cups cubed angel food cake
2 cups fresh raspberries
1 TBS. sugar

Spray bottom only of an 8-inch springform pan with nonstick spray coating; set aside. In a large bowl dissolve lemon gelatin in boiling water. Stir in thawed lemonade concentrate and evaporated skim milk. Cover and chill in refrigerator for 1-1 1/2 hours or until mixture mounds when spooned. After chilling, beat gelatin mixture with electric mixer for 5-6 minutes or until fluffy. Arrange angel food cake cubes in bottom of the springform pan. Pour gelatin mixture over cake cubes. Cover, chill for 4 hours or until firm. Meanwhile, in a small bowl stir together raspberries and sugar. Cover, chill at least 2 hours. To serve, cut torte into wedges, spoon raspberries on top. Serves 12.

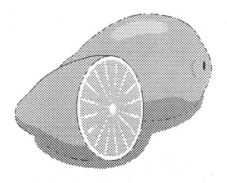

Katie's Black Russian Cake

1 18 1/2-oz. pkg. devils food cake mix
1 4-oz. pkg. instant chocolate pudding mix
4 eggs, beaten to blend
3/4 cup brewed strong coffee, room temperature
3/4 cup coffee liqueur
3/4 cup Creme de Cacao
1/2 cup vegetable oil
1 cup sifted powdered sugar
2 TBS. brewed strong coffee, room temperature
2 TBS. coffee liqueur
2 TBS. Creme de Cacao
additional powdered sugar

Preheat oven to 350º. Grease and lightly flour 10-inch bundt pan. Using electric mixer, blend first 7 ingredients at medium speed until batter forms. Pour into prepared pan. Bake until tester inserted in center comes out clean, about 45 minutes. Let cake cool in pan 10 minutes. Meanwhile, combine all remaining ingredients except additional powdered sugar in small bowl. Invert cake onto rack. Pierce top surface of cake with fork. Spoon glaze over. Cool completely. (Can be prepared 3 days ahead. Store in airtight container.) Dust cake with powdered sugar before serving.

 The very best shots are at the 19th hole.

Julie's Aunt Middy's Poppy Seed Cake

1 pkg. yellow cake mix
1 3.4-oz. pkg. yellow pudding
1 tsp. nutmeg
1 cup white wine
1/2 cup Crisco oil
4 eggs
1 tsp. vanilla
1 TBS. poppy seeds

Add 3 TBS. flour for high altitude. Mix all ingredients. Grease and flour a bundt pan. Pour all together in pan and bake at 350° for 45 minutes.

Tiller's Famous Chocolate Fudge

2 cups sugar
4 TBS. cocoa
1 cup whole milk
3 tsp. light Karo syrup

1 tsp. vanilla
6 TBS. butter
1 cup chopped pecans

Butter glass pan or dish. Blend sugar, cocoa, and 3/4 of the milk in large saucepan over medium heat. When it comes to a boil, add remaining 1/4 cup of milk. When it again comes to a boil, add Karo syrup then boil until it is reduced (about 30 minutes). When it forms a ball when dropped into a cup of cool water, add butter and vanilla; beat until it starts to turn lighter in color and hardens (about 20-25 minutes with electric beater). Quickly stir in nuts and pour into pan.

Three Layer Cookies

1/2 cup butter, melted
1 1/2 cups crushed graham crackers
2 1/2 cups (7-oz.) flaked coconut
1 can condensed milk (low fat)
12 oz. chocolate chips
1/2 cup crunchy peanut butter

Layer in 9x13-inch pan as follows:
1/2 cup butter (melted)
1 1/2 cups crushed graham crackers
2 1/2 cups flaked coconut
condensed milk (heated)

Cook 25 minutes at 325° until lightly browned. Cool slightly. Heat chocolate chips and peanut butter in a microwave until melted. Stir to mix. Pour over cookie mixture. Cool. Refrigerate overnight. Cut into squares.

Good shots are soon forgotten. Bad shots live on forever.

Sharon's Carrot Cake

2 cups sifted flour
2 tsp. baking powder
1 1/2 tsp. baking soda
1 tsp. salt
2 tsp. cinnamon
2 cups sugar
1 1/2 cups Wesson oil
4 eggs
2 cups finely grated carrots
1 13-oz. can crushed pineapple, drained
1 cup walnuts, chopped

Sift flour and measure. Sift a 2nd time with baking powder, soda, salt, cinnamon and sugar. Add oil and eggs and blend well. Reserve 2 TBS. pineapple for frosting. Add remaining pineapple and carrots to cake batter, stirring until thoroughly mixed. Fold in walnuts. Bake in three 9-inch greased and floured layer pans for 30 minutes at 350º. Frost when cool.

Frosting
1/2 cup butter
1 8-oz. pkg. cream cheese
1 tsp. vanilla
1 1-lb. box powdered sugar
2 TBS. well-drained crushed pineapple

Cream softened butter with cream cheese until smooth and well blended. Add vanilla. Gradually add powdered sugar, stirring until totally smooth. Stir in pineapple. This recipe makes a generous amount. You will use it for filling as well as for the top and sides of the cake.

George's Favorite Cheese Cake

Crust
4 oz. butter
1 1/2 cups graham crackers, ground
1/4 cup sugar
cinnamon to taste
1/4 cup almonds, chopped

Melt butter, add to graham crackers, sugar and cinnamon. Pack tightly in 10-inch cheesecake pan and bake at 375° for 6 minutes or until set. Let cool.

Filling
24 oz. cream cheese
1 cup sugar
4 eggs
1 TBS. vanilla
juice of 1 lemon
rind of 1/2 lemon

Cream together cream cheese and sugar, add eggs, one at a time, beating after each. Add vanilla and lemon juice and rind. Bake at 375° for 32 minutes. Let cool 10 minutes.

Topping
12 oz. sour cream
1/4 cup sugar
vanilla to taste

Cream together all ingredients, spread on top of cake and bake 6 minutes at 400°. Let cool 24 hours.

English Toffee

1/2 lb. butter
1 1/3 cups white sugar
1 TBS. Karo syrup (white)
1/2 cup chopped pecans
3 TBS. water

Topping
1/2 lb. Hershey Bar
1/2 cup chopped pecans

In a saucepan melt butter. Add Karo syrup, water, and sugar. Cook to 315° (on candy thermometer) stirring constantly over medium heat. Remove from heat. Add nuts quickly and spread in a 13x9x-inch pan that is well buttered. Cool thoroughly.

Melt 8 oz. milk chocolate bar in double boiler. Spread 1/2 of chocolate on top side of candy. Chop 1/2 cup pecans and spread half on top of chocolate that was spread on cooled candy. Cool thoroughly. Cover with waxpaper, turn over, and cover the other side with other half of chocolate and nuts. Cool. Break into small pieces. At high altitudes, add 2 more TBS. of water.

When putting remember, the hole is only as big as it looks to you.

Pumpkin Squares

2 cups sugar
4 eggs
2 cups pumpkin
1 cup salad oil
2 cups flour

2 tsp. baking powder
2 tsp. baking soda
1/2 tsp. cinnamon
1/2 tsp. nutmeg

Mix sugar, eggs, pumpkin, and salad oil. Sift and add flour, baking powder, baking soda, cinnamon and nutmeg. Put in greased 9x13-inch pan. Bake at 350° for 30 minutes or until toothpick comes out clean.

Icing
3 oz. cream cheese
3/4 stick butter

1 tsp. vanilla
2-3 cups powdered sugar

Mix icing ingredients and spread on cooled cake.

Mount Rose Apple Cake

Cake

4 TBS. butter
1 cup sugar
1 egg, beaten
3 apples, peeled and chopped
1 cup flour
1 tsp. baking soda

1/2 tsp. cinnamon
1/4 tsp. ground cloves
1/4 tsp. nutmeg
1/4 tsp. salt
1/2 cup chopped pecans

Cream butter and sugar. Add egg and beat well. Add remaining cake ingredients and mix until blended. Pour batter into a greased and floured 8-inch square pan and bake in preheated 350° oven for 45 minutes, or until cake tests done.

Frosting

2 TBS. butter, soft
1 cup powdered sugar
1/2 tsp. vanilla
1-2 TBS. apple juice

In a small bowl, beat together the butter, powdered sugar, vanilla and apple juice until consistency to spread on cake.

 Golf is 90 % mental, and 10 % mental.

Easy Chocolate Mousse

2 cups (12 oz.) semisweet chocolate chips
1 1/2 tsp. vanilla
1 1/2 cups whipping cream, heated to boiling
6 egg yolks
2 egg whites
whipped cream
pinch of salt

Combine chocolate, vanilla and salt in blender or food processor fitted with steel knife, and mix 30 seconds. Add heated cream and continue mixing 30 seconds more, or until chocolate is completely melted. Add egg yolks and mix about 5 seconds. Transfer to bowl and allow to cool. Beat egg whites until stiff peaks form. Gently fold into chocolate mixture. Place in serving bowl or wine glasses, cover with plastic wrap and chill. Serve with whipped cream if desired. Serves 4-6.

Honey Ginger Peach Salsa

3 cups fresh peaches, peeled, cut into 1/4-inch pieces (may use frozen)
1 jalapeño chili, unseeded, minced
1 tsp. minced fresh ginger
1 TBS. honey
2 TBS. fresh orange juice
1/2 tsp. cinnamon

Combine all ingredients. Let sit for 30 minutes for flavors to develop. Serve over ice cream.

Surprise Cake Roll

3/4 cup all purpose flour
1 tsp. baking powder
1 tsp. ground ginger
1/4 tsp. ground nutmeg
3 eggs
3/4 cup powdered sugar
3/4 cup granulated sugar
3/4 cup mashed cooked sweet potatoes
1 tsp. lemon juice
3/4 cup finely chopped pecans or walnuts
1 15-oz. part skim Ricotta cheese
1 tsp. vanilla
 skim milk
pecan halves

Grease and flour jelly roll pan. Stir together flour, baking powder, ginger and nutmeg. In a small bowl beat eggs at high speed 5 minutes until thick and lemon colored. Gradually add granulated sugar until dissolved. Stir in potatoes and lemon juice. Fold in dry ingredients. Spread evenly in pan. Sprinkle with nuts. Bake 375°, 12-15 minutes. Immediately loosen edges of cake and turn onto a towel. Sprinkle with 1 TBS. sifted powdered sugar. Roll up cake with towel. Cool seam side down on rack.

Filling
Mix cheese, powdered sugar, vanilla (add milk if too thick). Set aside 1/3 of filling. Unroll cake; spread with filling; roll up cake and place on serving platter.
Optional: Garnish top with remaining cheese mixture and pecan halves. Dust with sifted powdered sugar.

Earthquake Cake

1 cup chopped nuts, any kind, walnuts, pecans, etc.
1 cup angel cut coconut
1 pkg. German chocolate cake mix, per directions on box

Preheat oven to 350º. Grease and flour 9x13x2-inch sheet pan. Cover bottom of pan with chopped nuts and coconut. Prepare German chocolate cake mix and pour over nuts and coconut.

Topping
1 stick margarine
1 lb. powdered sugar
1 8-oz. pkg. cream cheese
1 tsp. vanilla

Mix together margarine, powdered sugar, cream cheese and vanilla. Drop mixture onto top of cake by spoonfuls. Do **not** spread, and do **not** touch edges of pan. Bake at 350º about 50 minutes. Serve with ice cream, frozen yogurt or Cool Whip.

It's not the tool...it's the fool with the tool.

Pecan Balls

1 cup soft butter or margarine
1/2 cup sifted powdered sugar
2 cups sifted all purpose flour
2 tsp. vanilla
1/4 tsp. salt
2 cups finely chopped pecans
powdered sugar (about 2 cups)

Gradually add 1/2 cup powdered sugar to butter. Cream thoroughly. Add vanilla. Add flour, salt and chopped pecans. Blend well. Chill in refrigerator. Shape into small balls about the size of marbles. Place on oiled cookie sheet. Bake in 350° oven for 15-18 minutes, until light brown. Remove from pan and roll hot cookies in sifted powdered sugar. Cool. Roll again in powdered sugar. Yields 3 dozen pecan balls.

Grandmother Warthan's Chess Pie

1 9-inch pie shell
1/4 lb. butter
1 1/2 cups sugar
1 TBS. white vinegar

1 1/2 TBS. cornmeal
3 eggs
1 tsp. vanilla extract

Mix the sugar and cornmeal very well. Melt butter and cool slightly. Add the sugar/cornmeal, vinegar, lightly beaten eggs, and vanilla. Pour into pie shell and bake at 425° for 10 minutes. Reduce heat to 275° and bake about 30 minutes longer or until set. Note: At high altitude, setting the oven temperature 25° higher yields the temperature called for in the recipe.

Angel Pie

4 eggs
1/2 tsp. cream of tartar
1 cup sugar
juice and rind of 1 lemon, grated
1/2 cup sugar
1/2 pint whipping cream
1 baked pie shell

Beat egg whites until foamy. Add cream of tartar and beat stiff. Add 1 cup sugar gradually until glossy. Put in well-buttered pie pan. Bake 275° for 20 minutes then 300° for 40 minutes. Cool. Beat yolks in top of double boiler. Add juice and rind of lemon; add 1/2 cup sugar; cook until thick. When cold, add 1/2 cup whipped cream. Put in baked pie shell. Put remaining whipped cream (sweetened) on top. Must sit in refrigerator overnight.

Pecan Tassies

Crust
3 oz. cream cheese
1 cup flour
1/2 cup butter

Filling
1 cup brown sugar
1 egg, slightly beaten
1/2 cup chopped pecans

Mix cream cheese, flour and butter with pastry cutter. Divide into 24 balls. Press into bottom and sides of muffin pan. Add filling and bake 20-25 minutes in 350° oven.

Chocolate Eclairs

1 16-oz. pkg. graham crackers
2 3 1/2-oz. pkgs. instant vanilla pudding mix
3 cups milk
1 8-oz. pkg. cream cheese, softened
1 8-oz. pkg. non-dairy whipped topping

Butter 13x9-inch pan, line with layer of graham crackers. Beat pudding with milk and cream cheese until stiff. Fold in whipped topping. Pour 1/2 of mixture over crackers. Place another layer of graham crackers on top and add remaining pudding mixture. Top with another layer of graham crackers. Drizzle or spoon frosting over top. Chill several hours. Makes 16 servings.

Frosting
2 1-oz. squares unsweetened chocolate
2 TBS. butter or margarine, softened
2 TBS. corn syrup **or** honey
3 TBS. milk
1 1/2 cups powdered sugar, sifted

Melt chocolate in top of double boiler over hot water. Beat in soft butter, corn syrup and milk. Stir in powdered sugar. Use immediately.

"There are now more golf clubs in the world than Gideon Bibles, more golf balls than missionaries and, if every golfer in the world, male and female, were laid end to end, I for one would leave them there."
Michael Parkinson, President, Anti-Golf Society.

St. Andrews Sticky Toffee Pudding

This traditional dessert was discovered while on a golfing trip to Scotland.

Pudding
3/4 cup sugar
1/4 cup (1/2 stick) unsalted butter at room temperature
1 large egg
1 1/2 cups all purpose flour
1 tsp. baking powder
1 1/4 cups boiling water
2 tsp. instant espresso powder **or** instant coffee powder
1 tsp. vanilla
1 tsp. baking soda

Preheat oven to 350º. Butter six custard cups. Using electric mixer, beat sugar and butter in large bowl until combined. Add egg and beat 2 minutes. Sift in flour and baking powder beating for 1 minute. Mix boiling water, espresso powder, vanilla and baking soda in a metal bowl. Add to butter mixture; beat until well blended. Divide batter among prepared custard cups. Bake until golden brown and tester inserted into center comes out clean, about 30 minutes. Transfer to rack; cool 10 minutes. Can use a 9-inch round baking dish instead of custard cups.

Sauce
1/3 cup firmly packed brown sugar
3 TBS. butter
2 TBS. whipping cream

Bring all ingredients to simmer in heavy small saucepan, stirring to dissolve sugar. Simmer 3 minutes, stirring occasionally. Preheat broiler. Pour sauce over warm pudding and broil until slightly caramelized about 2 minutes. Serve immediately.

A Proper Trifle

1 1/2 cups heavy cream
5 egg yolks
3 TBS. superfine sugar
1 1/2 tsp. cornstarch
5 cups broken pieces pound cake **or** sponge cake **or** lady fingers
raspberry jam
1/4 cup Sherry
1 1/2 cup frozen raspberries
1 banana (optional)

Topping
1/2 pint heavy cream, whipped **or** Cool Whip
1/4 cup toasted slivered almonds

To make the custard, heat the cream in a small saucepan, taking care that it does not scorch. In the meantime, whisk the egg yolks, sugar and cornstarch in a bowl. When the cream is hot, pour it into the bowl with the egg mixture, stirring constantly. Return the custard to the saucepan and stir constantly over low heat until thickened, but do not let it boil. Remove from the heat and cool. To assemble the trifle, spread the pieces of cake with a very thin layer of jam. Put the pieces in a large glass bowl. Sprinkle the Sherry, berries and bananas over the cake and stir. The berries do not have to be completely thawed. Drizzle the custard over the top; it will not cover completely, however you cover all with the whipped cream or Cool Whip. Sprinkle almonds on top. Cover and chill at least 4 hours. Serves 8-10.

Anita's Texas Chocolate Cake

1 cup melted butter
1 cup water
4 TBS. Hershey's cocoa
2 cups flour
2 cups sugar
1/2 tsp. salt
1 tsp. baking soda
2 eggs

1 cup sour cream
1/2 cup butter
4 1/2 TBS. Hershey's cocoa
6 TBS. milk
1 box powdered sugar
1 tsp. vanilla
1 cup chopped walnuts

Grease 11x17 cookie sheet with sides. Bring to boil butter, water and cocoa. Remove from heat. Add flour, sugar, salt and soda. Beat in eggs and sour cream. Pour onto cookie sheet. Bake at 375º for 15-20 minutes. While cake is baking mix in pan, butter, cocoa, and milk. Heat until melted. Add powdered sugar, vanilla and nuts. Ice cake while still a little warm.

Peggy's Forgotten Cookies

2 egg whites
3/4 cup sugar
1 cup nuts, chopped
1 small pkg. chocolate chips

Beat 2 egg whites until very stiff; add 3/4 cup sugar gradually while still beating; fold in 1 cup chopped nuts and one small package chocolate chips; drop on cookie sheet and put in preheated 350º oven. Turn oven to off and leave for 4 hours. Don't open door during this time.

Oatmeal Cake

1 cup minute oats
1 1/2 cups boiling water
1 cup brown sugar
1/2 cup white sugar
1/2 cup shortening
2 eggs, beaten
1 tsp. soda
1/2 tsp. salt
1 tsp. cinnamon
1 1/2 cups flour
2 TBS. sour cream

Pour water over oats and let stand for 10 minutes. Cream sugar, shortening and add beaten eggs and beat well. Sift dry ingredients together. Add, alternating with oats. Bake in 8x12-inch pan at 375° for 35 minutes.

Oatmeal Topping
1 stick margarine, melted
1/2 cup brown sugar
1/4 cup cream
1 cup nuts (or 5 1/2-oz. bag)
1 cup coconut
1 tsp. vanilla

Mix together and spread mixture on cake as soon as the cake is taken from the oven. Put under broiler until coconut is brown. Watch very closely as it burns easily.

Lemon Pie

1 9-inch Best Ever Pastry Shell
1 cup sugar
3 TBS. cornstarch
4 TBS. butter
1 tsp. freshly grated lemon peel
1/4 cup fresh lemon juice
3 large egg yolks, beaten

1 cup whole milk
1 cup sour cream
sweetened whipped cream
sugared lemon slices
chopped walnuts

In a saucepan, mix sugar, cornstarch, butter, lemon peel, lemon juice, egg yolks and milk; stir and cook until thick, about 5 to 10 minutes. Cool. Fold in sour cream. Pour into baked pastry shell. Refrigerate at least 12 hours. Serve with sweetened whipped cream, garnish with sugared lemon slices and/or chopped walnuts. Serves 6-8.

Best Ever Pie Crust

3 cups all purpose flour
1 1/2 cups Crisco
1 tsp. salt

1 tsp. white vinegar
6 TBS. water
1 egg

With pastry blender, combine flour, Crisco and salt until mixture resembles coarse meal. In small bowl, mix egg, vinegar and water; add to flour mixture, mixing only until dough holds together in a ball. Refrigerate for 1 hour. Roll out on waxed paper or pastry cloth. Turn onto lightly greased pie plate. Trim to a 1-inch overhang and flute edges. Prick all over with a fork. Bake at 400° for 11 minutes or until golden brown. Makes 2 10-inch deep-dish or 3 9-inch shells.

Pumpkin Mincemeat Pie

At holiday parties, the members of this family always wanted both a piece of pumpkin pie and mincemeat pie. This chef's creation solves that problem without doubling the work.

1 16-oz. can pumpkin pie mix, prepared as directed on can
1 27-oz. jar mincemeat
pumpkin pie spice to taste
1 10-inch deep dish frozen **or** homemade pie crust

Line a 10-inch deep dish pie pan with homemade or frozen prepared pie crust. Prepare pumpkin according to directions on the can. Fill pie 1/2 full with mincemeat on the bottom and 1/2 full with pumpkin mix on the top of the mincemeat and cook at 425° for 15 minutes then 350° for 40-50 minutes or until pumpkin does not stick to a knife. This quantity of ingredients will also make 2 8-inch average depth pies. Leftover mincemeat and pumpkin mix can be cooked in custard cups.

Hot Fudge Sauce

2 squares bitter chocolate
1 cup sugar
1 small can unsweetened evaporated milk

1 TBS. butter
1 tsp. vanilla

Combine chocolate, sugar, and evaporated milk in double boiler and cook stirring occasionally for 30 minutes or until thick. Add 1 TBS. butter, 1 tsp. vanilla and stir. To thin, add milk or water. Serve hot fudge sauce on ice cream.

Mocha Pots de Creme

2 TBS. cocoa
2 TBS. instant coffee
2 cups skim milk

6 egg yolks
1 TBS. liquid sweetener
1 tsp. vanilla

Preheat oven to 325º. Combine cocoa and coffee in saucepan. Gradually stir in skim milk; bring just to a boil. Beat yolks until thick and lemon colored; blend in hot mocha mixture. Blend in sweetener and vanilla. Pour into 6 half-cup creme pots or small custard cups. Set pots in pan of hot water; cover pan with foil and bake about 30 minutes, or until a knife inserted near the center comes out clean. Chill well before serving. Garnish, if desired, with coconut. Serves 6.

Cranberry Mousse

1 3-oz. pkg. raspberry Jell-O
1 cup Ocean Spray Cranberry Juice
1 16-oz. can cranberry sauce

chopped walnuts
2 cups non-dairy whipped topping

In a saucepan bring cranberry juice cocktail to a boil; remove from heat; stir in gelatin until dissolved. In a bowl, beat cranberry sauce with electric mixer on high 1 minute. Stir into gelatin mixture, chill in refrigerator 2 1/2 hours until thickened, but NOT set. Fold in walnuts and whipped topping until mixture is thoroughly blended. Chill until ready to serve.

Almond Tart

Crust

1 1/3 cups all purpose flour
3 TBS. sugar
1/2 tsp. salt
grated zest of 1 lemon or orange

8 TBS. cold unsalted butter, cut into bits
1 large egg, lightly beaten
1 tsp. vanilla extract

In a large bowl, combine the flour, sugar, salt and zest. With a pastry blender or fork, blend in the butter until the mixture resembles coarse meal. Add egg and vanilla and toss the mixture with a fork until the egg is incorporated. Gather the dough together and shape it into a ball. Wrap it in plastic wrap and chill for at least 1 hour or overnight.

Almond Tart

3 large eggs, room temperature
1/4 cup sugar
1 8-oz. can almond paste
1/2 cup all purpose flour

3/4 cup cherry or raspberry jam
1/2 cup sliced almonds
confectioners sugar

On a lightly floured surface, roll dough into 11-inch circle, 1/8-inch thick. Press dough into 9 or 10-inch fluted tart pan with removable bottom. Trim all but 1/2-inch border of dough. Fold excess dough in against the inside of the pan and press it into place. Chill for 30 minutes. Preheat oven to 350º. In a medium bowl beat eggs until foamy. Gradually beat in sugar, crumble almond paste into egg mixture and beat until smooth. Fold in flour. Spread jam over bottom of prepared shell. Spread almond mixture over jam. Sprinkle with sliced almonds. Bake in bottom half of oven for 30-35 minutes until golden. Cool for 10 minutes on wire rack. Remove pan rim and cool tart completely. Just before serving sprinkle with confectioners sugar.

Chocolate Squares

1 cup butter
2 1/2 cups graham cracker crumbs
sugar
5 TBS. cocoa
1 egg, beaten
1 cup coconut

1/2 cup chopped walnuts
2 cups confectioners sugar
5-7 squares bitter chocolate
3 TBS. vanilla pudding
3 TBS. milk

Melt 1/2 cup butter; add 2 1/2 cups graham cracker crumbs. In a bowl mix 1/4 cup sugar, 5 TBS. cocoa, 1 beaten egg, 1 cup coconut and 1/2 cup chopped walnuts. Mix with cracker crumbs and press into pan (approx. 10"x14").

Topping
Cream 1/2 cup butter with 3 TBS. vanilla pudding, 3 TBS. milk and 2 cups confectioners sugar. Spread on top of crumbs. Melt 5-7 squares of the bitter chocolate and pour over all. Refrigerate, cut in squares and serve. Store in refrigerator. Note: Scoring the chocolate before it hardens completely makes cutting easier.

Wilson's Law: Balls you buy for 10% off are available the next day for half price.

Rainbow Pie

Pie Crust
1 1/3 cups flour
1/4 lb. butter
1/4 cup ice water

Cut butter into 8 pieces. In a Cuisinart process butter and flour until mixture has the consistency of coarse meal. With machine running, pour ice water in a steady stream through feeding tube. In 20-50 seconds a ball will form. This dough may be used immediately. Roll one half dough; use for bottom crust. Put fork holes all over crust; bake at 425° for about 7 minutes.

Filling
3-4 ripe firm pears, sliced, cored, and peeled
1 box fresh blueberries (about 1 1/2 cups)
4 large ripe peaches
    or 3-4 mangos
    or 2 cups pitted apricots
    or combination of all three
1 cup brown sugar
3 TBS. tapioca
1/2 tsp. fresh ground nutmeg
dash of salt

In a large mixing bowl put brown sugar, tapioca, nutmeg and salt. Mix. Add all fruit and mix well. In the half baked pie shell pour all the fruit. Roll out remaining pie crust and cut in 1/2-inch strips. Make a simple lattice top. Bake at 425° for 1 hour. Serves 8.

Prune Spice Cake

1 cup sugar
1 cup shortening
1/2 cup sour cream
2 eggs
1 cup prune pulp
1 1/2 cups cake flour

1 1/2 tsp. soda
1 tsp. cinnamon
3/4 tsp. cloves
1/2 tsp. salt
1/2 cup broken walnuts

Sift one cup sugar; beat until soft 1 cup shortening (this may be reduced to 3/4 or 1/2 cupful) and add sugar gradually. Blend these ingredients until they are light and creamy. Beat in one at a time 2 eggs. Beat in 1 cup prune pulp (use 16-oz. can Sunsweet ready to serve prunes; pit; put in 1 cup measuring cup; add enough juice to make exactly one cup). Sift before measuring 1 1/2 cups cake flour. Resift with soda, cinnamon, cloves, salt. Add the sifted ingredients in 3 parts to the butter mixture alternately with thirds of 1/2 cup sour cream (can use soured whipping cream, sour cream or buttermilk). Stir in 1/2 cup broken walnuts; pour batter into 2 greased 9-inch layer pans or a 9x13 pan. Bake the layers for 25 minutes in a 375º oven. Bake the 9x13 loaf cake at 350º and slightly increase the heat for about one hour. Top with whipped cream, ice cream, marshmallow and coconut custard or serve plain. Serves 8-10.

If you really want to get better at golf, go back and take it up at a much earlier age.

Pumpkin Squares

Crust
1 cup flour
1/2 cup uncooked quick cooking oats
1/2 cup brown sugar
1/2 cup butter

Combine until crumbly. Press into buttered 9x13-inch pan. Bake at 350° for 15 minutes.

Filling
2 cups canned pumpkin
1 large can evaporated milk
2 eggs
3/4 cup sugar
1 tsp. cinnamon
1/4 tsp. cloves

Combine well. Pour into crust. Bake 20 minutes.

Topping
1/2 cup chopped pecans
1/2 cup brown sugar
2 TBS. butter

Mix together. It will be crumbly. Sprinkle over filling. Bake an additional 20-25 minutes more until filling is set.

The Incline Village Golf Club wishes to thank its members and their friends who contributed to this book:

Dorothy Anderson
Susie Anderson
Joyce Anderson
George Archer
Bev Atherton
Dick Atherton
George Bayer
Mary Ann Bayer
Susie Maxwell Berning
Trary Bishop
Charlie Bock
Lois Boudwin
Valerie Bowles
Dotti Brewer
Carol Buck
Janusz Clark
Julie Clark
Rockee Coalson
Alice Colling
Alyce Craft
Peggy Crayton
George Croom
Sharon Croom
Lee Cunningham
Katie Dimick
Helen DiZio
Steve DiZio
Margie Eccles
Marta Figueras-Dotti
Ellie Gibson
Marilyn Gilbert
Helen Gotchy

Jane Graff
John Hughes
Julie Inkster
Hale Irwin
Peggy Jones
Barbara Kallestad
Hugh Kelley
Barbara Kerber
Betsy King
Mabelle Kiper
Marian Kopf
GJ Kosanke
Blanche Latshaw
George Lee
Karen Leonardini
Alice Logan
Shiela Lonie
Susy Madigan
Thelma Maltz
Esther McCammon
Gayle McGough
Kay Mc Mahon
Marisa Menning
Julie Molloy
Ione Monagan
Diana Olson
Chuck Otto
Jeanne Otto
Arnold Palmer
Katie Peterson-Parker
Bill Platt
Carol Platt

Bonnie Porter
Jeff Quinn
Shelly Quinn
Jean Rowley
Dale Shaw
Frances Schafer
Erin Scheller
Virginia Schmid
Margaret Schmidt
Dan Schwartz
Irene Schwartz
Patty Sheehan
Louise Shulman
Cynthia Silman
Joe Silman
Panchita Simon
Patty Stampfli
Ron Stanger
Marge Steil
Jean Teipner
Martie Teipner
Ann Tiller
Harold Tiller
Sharon Valerio
Jutta Wayland
Gene Weatherly
Thryza Weatherly
Jeanne Weiskopf
Tom Weiskopf
Lori West
Peggy Winner
Shelly Godeken-Wright

Index

Cookbook Order Form

Tea Times Press
PO Box 3414
Incline Village, NV 89450

Please send me _____ copies of Tea Times at Lake Tahoe @ $14.95 per copy plus $3.00

per copy for postage and handling. Enclosed is my check or money order for $_____.

_____
Name

_____
Address

_____
City   State   Zip Code

Please make checks payable to: Tea Times at Lake Tahoe.

Cookbook Order Form

Tea Times Press
PO Box 3414
Incline Village, NV 89450

Please send me _____ copies of Tea Times at Lake Tahoe @ $14.95 per copy plus $3.00

per copy for postage and handling. Enclosed is my check or money order for $_____.

_____
Name

_____
Address

_____
City   State   Zip Code

Please make checks payable to: Tea Times at Lake Tahoe.